SUSE Linux Enterprise Desktop 12 - GNOME User Guide

A catalogue record for this book is available from the Hong Kong Public Libraries.

Published in Hong Kong by Samurai Media Limited.

Email: info@samuraimedia.org

ISBN 978-988-8406-57-9

Contents

About This Guide

This manual introduces you to the GNOME graphical desktop environment as implemented in SUSE® Linux Enterprise Desktop, and shows you how to configure it to meet your personal needs and preferences. It also introduces you to several programs and services. It is intended for users who have some experience using a graphical desktop environment such as Macintosh*, Windows*, or other Linux desktops.

The manual is divided into two parts:

Introduction

Get to know your GNOME desktop, learn how to cope with basic and daily tasks using the central GNOME applications and various small utilities. Get an overview of the possibilities that GNOME offers for modifying and individualizing the desktop according to your needs and wishes. Learn how to use assistive technologies to improve accessibility in case of vision or mobility impairment.

Connectivity, Files and Resources

Find vital information concerning the management and exchange of data on your system: how to share files on the network and how to use an integrated collaboration environment, how to effectively search for data, and how to manage printers and back up your data.

LibreOffice

Introduces the LibreOffice suite, including Writer, Calc, Impress, Base, Draw, and Math.

Information Management

Get to know the e-mailing and calendaring software provided by your product. Learn how to use protected information transfer by signing and encrypting your documents or mails.

Communication and Collaboration

Stay in contact with others and communicate via network connections using Instant Messaging or Voice over IP.

Internet

Search for information on the Web with browsers combining the latest browsing and security technologies. Use file transfer clients to transfer data from the Internet.

Graphics

Get to know GIMP, an image manipulation program that meets the needs of both amateurs and professionals.

Multimedia

Get introduced to your desktop's applications for playing movies. Learn how to create data or audio CDs and DVDs for archiving your data.

Many chapters in this manual contain links to additional documentation resources. These include additional documentation that is available on the system and documentation available on the Internet.

For an overview of the documentation available for your product and the latest documentation updates, refer to http://www.suse.com/doc or to the following section.

1 Available Documentation

We provide HTML and PDF versions of our books in different languages. The following manuals for users and administrators are available for this product:

Article "Installation Quick Start"

Lists the system requirements and guides you step-by-step through the installation of SUSE Linux Enterprise Desktop from DVD, or from an ISO image.

Book "Deployment Guide"

Shows how to install single or multiple systems and how to exploit the product inherent capabilities for a deployment infrastructure. Choose from various approaches, ranging from a local installation or a network installation server to a mass deployment using a remote-controlled, highly-customized, and automated installation technique.

Book "Administration Guide"

Covers system administration tasks like maintaining, monitoring and customizing an initially installed system.

Book "Security Guide"

Introduces basic concepts of system security, covering both local and network security aspects. Shows how to use the product inherent security software like AppArmor or the auditing system that reliably collects information about any security-relevant events.

Book "System Analysis and Tuning Guide"

> An administrator's guide for problem detection, resolution and optimization. Find how to inspect and optimize your system by means of monitoring tools and how to efficiently manage resources. Also contains an overview of common problems and solutions and of additional help and documentation resources.

GNOME User Guide

> Introduces the GNOME desktop of SUSE Linux Enterprise Desktop. It guides you through using and configuring the desktop and helps you perform key tasks. It is intended mainly for end users who want to make efficient use of GNOME as their default desktop.

Find HTML versions of most product manuals in your installed system under `/usr/share/doc/manual` or in the help centers of your desktop. Find the latest documentation updates at http://www.suse.com/doc where you can download PDF or HTML versions of the manuals for your product.

2 Feedback

Several feedback channels are available:

Bugs and Enhancement Requests

> For services and support options available for your product, refer to http://www.suse.com/support/.
>
> To report bugs for a product component, go to https://scc.suse.com/support/requests, log in, and click *Create New*.

User Comments

> We want to hear your comments about and suggestions for this manual and the other documentation included with this product. Use the User Comments feature at the bottom of each page in the online documentation or go to http://www.suse.com/doc/feedback.html and enter your comments there.

Mail

> For feedback on the documentation of this product, you can also send a mail to doc-team@suse.de. Make sure to include the document title, the product version and the publication date of the documentation. To report errors or suggest enhancements, provide a concise description of the problem and refer to the respective section number and page (or URL).

3 Documentation Conventions

The following typographical conventions are used in this manual:

- /etc/passwd: directory names and file names

- *placeholder*: replace *placeholder* with the actual value

- PATH: the environment variable PATH

- **ls**, --help: commands, options, and parameters

- user: users or groups

- Alt , Alt – F1 : a key to press or a key combination; keys are shown in uppercase as on a keyboard

- *File*, *File > Save As*: menu items, buttons

- *Dancing Penguins* (Chapter *Penguins*, ↑Another Manual): This is a reference to a chapter in another manual.

I Introduction

1 Getting Started with the GNOME Desktop

This section describes the conventions, layout, and common tasks of the GNOME desktop as implemented in your product.

GNOME is an easy-to-use graphical interface that can be customized to meet your needs and personal preferences. This section describes the default configuration of GNOME. If you or your system administrator modify the defaults, some aspect might be different, such as appearance or key combinations.

 Note: Included Session Configurations

> Some versions of SUSE Linux Enterprise ship with as many as three different session configurations based on GNOME. These are GNOME, GNOME Classic, and SLE Classic. The version described here is the default configuration of SUSE Linux Enterprise Desktop called SLE Classic.

1.1 Logging In

In general, all users must authenticate—unless *Auto Login* is enabled for a specific user. In this case, a particular user will be logged in automatically when the system starts. This can save some time, especially if a computer is used by a single person. It may impact account security. Auto Login can be enabled or disabled during installation or at any time using the YaST User and Group Management module. For more information, refer to *Book "Deployment Guide", Chapter 8 "Managing Users with YaST"*.

If your computer is running in a network environment and you are not the only person using the machine, you are usually prompted to enter your user name and password when you start the system. If you did not set up the system and user account yourself, check with your system administrator for your user name and password.

PROCEDURE 1.1: NORMAL LOGIN

1. If your name is listed, click it.
   If your name is not listed, click *Not listed?*. Then enter your user name and click *Next.*

2. Enter your password and click *Sign in.*

1.1.1 Switching the Session Type Before Logging In

If you want to try one of the additional GNOME session configurations or try another desktop environment, follow the steps below.

1. On the login screen, click your user name or enter it, as you normally would.

2. To change the session type, click the cog wheel icon. A menu appears.

3. From the menu, select one of the entries. Depending on your configuration there may be different choices, but the default selection is as follows.

   GNOME

   A GNOME 3 configuration that is very close to the upstream design. It focuses on interrupting users as little as possible. However, starting applications and switching between them works differently from many other desktop operating systems. It uses a single panel at the top of the screen.

   GNOME Classic

   A GNOME 3 configuration that is designed to appeal to former users of GNOME 2. The desktop has two panels, one at the top and another at the bottom.

   IceWM

   A very basic desktop designed to use little resources. It can be used as a fallback, if other options do not work or are slow.

   SLE Classic *(default)*

   The default desktop of SUSE Linux Enterprise, designed to appeal to users of older versions of SUSE Linux Enterprise and users of Microsoft* Windows*. This desktop is a GNOME 3 configuration and uses a single panel that is placed at the bottom of the screen.

4. Enter your password into the text box, then click *Sign In*.

After switching to another session type once, the chosen session will become your default session. To switch back, repeat the steps above.

1.1.2 Assistive Tools

In the top right corner, there are status icons and the assistive technologies menu. By clicking the status icons, open a menu that allows you to set the sound volume and restart or power off the machine.

1.2 Desktop Basics

The GNOME desktop appears after you first log in. It displays a panel at the bottom showing the following elements (from left to right):

Applications menu

Click *Applications* in the left corner to open a menu with all the installed programs. These are classified under different categories for a better overview. Sub-items open automatically as soon as you place the mouse above them.

Click *Activities Overview* in the bottom part of the *Applications* menu to open Activities Overview where you can start programs and manage those already running.

The Activity Overview is described further in *Section 1.2.1, "Activities Overview"*.

Places menu

Click *Places* to open a menu with shortcuts to your personal directories, connected storage media, and network resources.

Task switcher

All applications currently open on the desktop (on the active workspace) appear in the middle part of the panel. You can bring these applications to the foreground by clicking their names.

Notification indicator *(not always visible)*

When there are notifications, for example, for new chat or e-mail messages or concerning system updates, an indicator will appear. The indicator is a blue circle with the number of available notifications displayed in the middle. Click the indicator to open the Message Tray where you can interact with all the notifications.

Workspace switcher

This menu lets you select a workspace (also called a virtual desktop) to work on. This feature can help you work with many windows. For example, you could move windows needed for one project to workspace 1 and windows needed for another project to workspace 2.

Date and time

The current day of the week and time are shown to the right from the workspace switcher. Click it to open a menu where you can access a calendar and adjust date and time settings.

Status icons

In the right corner of the panel, icons showing the current status of the network connection, sound volume and power/battery status are displayed.

Click the icons to open a menu where you can adjust sound volume, display brightness, network connection, and power settings. Click the name to display the options for logging out or for switching to another user.

The three icons in the lower part of the menu allow you to, from left to right, open the GNOME settings dialog, lock the screen, and power off or restart your computer.

1.2.1   Activities Overview

Activities Overview is a full screen mode that comprises all the ways in which you can switch from one activity to another. It shows previews of all open windows and icons for favorite and running applications. It also integrates searching and browsing functionality.

1.2.1.1   Opening the Activities Overview

There are multiple ways to open the Activities Overview:

- Open the *Applications* menu on the bottom panel and select *Activities Overview*.

- Press `Meta` .

- Forcefully move the mouse cursor to the top left corner (the so-called *hot corner*).

1.2.1.2   Using the Activities Overview

In the following, the most important parts of the Activities Overview are explained.

Dash

The Dash is the bar positioned on the center left. It contains favorite applications and all applications with open windows. If you move the mouse pointer over one of the icons, GNOME will display the name of the corresponding application nearby. A light glow indicates that the application is running and has at least one open window.

Right-clicking an icon opens a menu which offers different actions depending on the associated program. Using *Add to Favorites*, you can place the application icon permanently in Dash. To remove a program icon from Dash, select *Remove from Favorites*. To rearrange an icon, use the mouse to drag it to a new position.

Search box

On the top, there is a search box that you can use to find applications, settings and files in your home directory.

To search, you do not need to click the search box. You can begin typing directly after opening Activity Overview. Search starts immediately, you do not need to press `Enter`.

Workspace selector

On the right, there is an overview of available workspaces. To switch to the selected desktop, click the preview of it.

To move a window from one workspace to another, drag a window preview from one workspace preview to another.

1.2.2 Starting Programs

To start a program, you have several options:

- In the bottom panel, click *Applications* and select the desired program from the hierarchical menu.

- Open the Activities Overview by pressing `Meta`. Now click an application icon or search for an application. If you do not know the exact application name, you can search for generic category names such as "image editor".
  Further information about the activities overview can be found in *Section 1.2.1, "Activities Overview"*.

- If you know the exact command to start the program, you can press `Alt`-`F2`, enter the command into the dialog and press `Enter`.
  Note that the only button displayed in the window is labeled *Close* and will indeed close the window.

1.3 Pausing or Finishing Your Session

When you have finished using the computer, there are multiple ways to finish the session. Which one is right in a given situation depends on how long you will be away and whether you are worried about energy consumption, among other things.

- **Locking the Computer.** Pause your session, but keep the computer on. Make sure that nobody can look at or change your work while you are away on a break. Other users can log in and work in the meantime. Other users can shut down the computer, but a prompt will warn them that you are still logged in.

- **Logging Out.** Finish the current session, but leave the computer on, so other users can log in.

- **Shutting Down.** Finish the current session and turn off the computer.

- **Restarting.** Finish the current session and restart the computer. Restarting is necessary to apply some system updates.

- **Suspending the Computer.** Pause your session and put the computer in a state where it consumes a minimal amount of energy. Suspend mode can be configured to lock your screen, so nobody can look at or change your work. Waking up the computer is generally much quicker than a full computer start.
  This mode is also known as suspend-to-RAM, sleep or standby mode.

1.3.1 Locking the Screen

To lock the screen, click the status icons on the right of the main panel and click the padlock icon. When you lock your screen, at first a curtain with a clock will appear. After some time the screen turns black. To unlock the screen, move the mouse or press a key to display the locked screen dialog. Enter your password, then press Enter to unlock the screen.

1.3.2 Logging Out or Switching Users

1. Click the status icons on the right of the main panel to open the menu.

2. Click your user name.

3. Select one of the following options:

Log Out

> Logs you out of the current session and returns you to the Login screen.

Switch User

> Suspends your session, allowing another user to log in and use the computer.

1.3.3 Restarting or Shutting Down the Computer

1. Click the status icons on the right of the main panel to open the menu.

2. Click the power off icon in the lower right part of the menu.

3. Select one of the following options:

Power Off

> Logs you out of the current session, then turns off the computer.

Restart

> Logs you out of the current session, then restarts the computer.

1.3.4 Suspending the Computer

1. Click the status icons on the right of the main panel to open the menu.

2. Hold `Alt` pressed. The power off icon in the lower right part of the menu turns into a pause icon. Click the pause icon.

2 Working with Your Desktop

In this chapter you will learn how to work with files and burn CDs. You will also find out how to perform regular tasks with your desktop.

2.1 Managing Files and Directories

Use GNOME Files (formerly known as Nautilus) to view and create directories and documents on your computer and in the network. You can also use GNOME Files to create CDs of your data.

You can open GNOME Files in multiple ways:

- Click *Applications* › *Accessories* › *Files*.
- Open the Activities Overview and search for `files`.
- On the desktop, double-click *Home*.
- Open the *Places* menu and select any entry, such as *Home*.

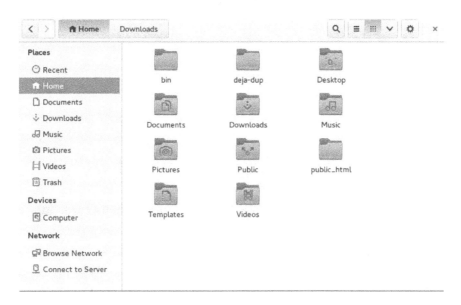

FIGURE 2.1: FILE MANAGER

The elements of the GNOME Files window include the following:

Toolbar

> The toolbar contains back and forward buttons, the path bar, a search function, elements to let you change the layout of the content area, and the application menu.

Menu

> The menu is the last icon on the toolbar, labeled with a cog wheel icon. It lets you perform many tasks, such as opening the preferences dialog, creating a new directory or opening a new window or tab.

Sidebar

> The sidebar lets you navigate between often-used directories and external or network storage devices. To display or hide the sidebar, press `F9`.

Content Area

> Displays files and directories.
>
> Use the icons in the top right part of the window to switch between list and grid icon view. The menu to the right of these icons can be used to further customize the view.

Context Menus

> Open a context menu by right-clicking inside the content area. The items in this menu depend on where you right-click.
>
> For example, if you right-click a file or directory, you can select items related to the file or directory. If you right-click the background of a content area, you can select items related to the display of items in the content area.

Floating Statusbar

> The floating statusbar appears when a file is selected. It displays the file name and size.

2.1.1   Key Combinations

The following table lists a selection of key combinations of GNOME Files.

TABLE 2.1: GNOME FILES KEY COMBINATIONS

Key Combination	Description
`Alt`-`←` / `Alt`-`→`	Go backward/go forward.
`Alt`-`↑`	Open the parent directory.
`←`, `→`, `↑`, `↓`	Select an item.
`Alt`-`↓` or `Enter`	Open an item.

Key Combination	Description
`Alt`–`Enter`	Open an item's *Properties* dialog.
`Shift`–`Alt`–`↓`	Open an item and close the current directory.
`Ctrl`–`L`	Transform the path bar from a button view to a text box. Exit this mode by pressing `Enter` (go to the location) or `Esc` (to remain in the current directory).
`/`	Transform the path bar from a button view to a text box and replace the current path with `/`.
`Alt`–`Home`	Open your home directory.
Any number or letter key	Start a search within the current directories and their subdirectories. The character you pressed is used as the first character of the search term. Search happens as you type, you do not need to press `Enter`.
`Ctrl`–`T`	Start a search within the current directories and their subdirectories. The character you pressed is used as the first character of the search term. Search happens as you type, you do not need to press `Enter`.

2.1.2   Compressing Files or Directories

Sometimes, it is useful to archive or compress files, for example:

- You want to attach an entire directory, including its subdirectories, to an e-mail.

- You want to attach a large file to an e-mail.

- You want to save space on your hard disk and have files you rarely use.

In all these cases, you can create a compressed file, such as a ZIP file, which can contain multiple original files. How much smaller the compressed version is than the original depends on the file type. Many video, image and office document formats are already compressed and will only become marginally smaller.

1. In the GNOME Files content area, right-click the directory you want to archive, then click *Compress*.

2. Accept the default archive file name or provide a new one.

3. Select a file extension from the drop-down box.

   - `.zip` files are supported on most operating systems, including Windows*.

   - `.tar.gz` files are compatible with most Linux* and Unix* systems.

   - `.7z` files usually offer better compression ratios than other formats, but are not as widely supported.

4. Specify a location for the archive file, then click *Create*.

To extract an archived file, right-click the file, then select *Extract Here*. You can also double-click the compressed file to open it and see which files are included.

For more information on compressed files, see *Section 2.10, "Creating, Displaying, and Decompressing Archives"*.

2.1.3 Burning a CD/DVD

If your system has a CD or DVD writer, you can use GNOME Files to burn CDs and DVDs. If you want to burn an audio CD or need more control over the result, see *Chapter 20, Brasero: Burning CDs and DVDs*.

1. Open GNOME Files.

2. Insert a blank medium.

3. Find the files you want to add to the medium and drag them to the sidebar item called *Blank CD-R Disc*. (The label may read slightly differently, depending on the type of medium you inserted.) When your mouse pointer is over the sidebar item, a small + should appear next to the pointer.

4. When you have dragged all files onto the sidebar item *Blank CD-R Disc*, click it.

5. Provide a name next to *Disc Name* or keep the proposal.

6. Click *Write to Disc*.

7. In the appearing dialog *CD/DVD Creator*, make sure the right medium is selected. Then click *Burn*.
   The files are burned to the disc. This can take a few minutes, depending on the amount of data being burned and the speed of your burner.

8. After the medium has been burned, it will be ejected from the drive. In the window *CD/DVD Creator*, you can click *Close*.

To burn an ISO disc image, first insert a medium, then double-click the ISO file in GNOME Files. In the dialog *Image Burning Setup*, click *Burn*.

2.1.4   Creating a Bookmark

Use the bookmarks feature in GNOME Files to quickly jump to your favorite directories from the sidebar.

1. Switch to the directory for which you want to create a bookmark in the content area.

2. Click the cog wheel icon, then select *Bookmark this Location* from the menu.
   The bookmark now appears in the sidebar, with the directory name as the bookmark name.

3. If you want, you can change the name of the bookmark. This does not affect the name of the bookmarked directory itself. To change the name, right-click the new sidebar item and select *Rename*.

4. If you want, you can change the order in which the bookmarks are displayed. To reorder, click a bookmark and drag it to the desired location.

To switch to a bookmarked directory, click the appropriate sidebar item.

2.1.5   File Manager Preferences

Open the file manager preferences by clicking the cog wheel icon and selecting *Preferences*.

2.1.6 Accessing Remote Files

You can use GNOME Files to access files on remote servers. For more information, see *Chapter 5, Accessing Network Resources*.

2.2 Accessing Removable Media

To access CDs/DVDs or flash disks, insert or attach the medium. An icon for the medium is automatically created on the desktop. For many types of removable media, a GNOME Files window pops up automatically. If GNOME Files does not open, double-click the icon for that drive on the desktop to view the contents. In GNOME Files, you will see an item for the medium in the sidebar.

 ### Warning: Unmount to Prevent Data Loss

Do not physically remove flash disks immediately after using them. Even when the system does not indicate that data is being written, the drive may not be finished with a previous operation.

On the desktop or in the sidebar of GNOME Files, right-click the icon for the medium and select *Safely Remove Drive* or *Unmount*.

2.3 Searching for Files

There are multiple ways to search for files or directories. In all cases, the search will be performed on file and directory names. Searching by file size, modification date and other properties is not possible in the preinstalled graphical tools. Such searches are easier to do on the command line.

Using GNOME Files

In GNOME Files, navigate to the directory from which you want to start the search. Then start typing the search term.

Using the Activities Overview

Open the Activities Overview by pressing Meta . Then start typing the search term. The search will be performed within your home directory.

Using the Desktop Search application

Click *Applications* › *Accessories* › *Desktop Search*. Enter the search term in the text box *Search*. The search will be performed within your home directory.

2.4 Copying Text Between Applications

Copy and paste works the same as in other operating systems. First select the text, so that it appears highlighted, usually in blue. Then press `Ctrl`–`C`. Now move the keyboard focus to the right position. Finally, to insert the text, press `Ctrl`–`V`.

To copy or paste in the terminal, additionally press `Shift` together with the above key combinations.

An alternative way of using copy and paste is described in the following. First select the text. To paste the text, middle-click over the position where you want the text to be pasted. As soon as you make another selection, the text from the original selection will be replaced in the clipboard.

When copying information between programs, you must keep the source program open and paste the text before closing it. When a program closes, any content from that application that is on the clipboard is lost.

2.5 Managing Internet Connections

To surf the Internet or send and receive e-mail messages, you must have configured an Internet connection with YaST. Depending on your environment, in YaST select whether to use NetworkManager. In GNOME, you can then establish Internet connections with NetworkManager as described in *Book "Administration Guide", Chapter 22 "Using NetworkManager", Section 22.3 "Configuring Network Connections"*.

For a list of criteria to help you decide whether to use NetworkManager, refer to *Book "Administration Guide", Chapter 22 "Using NetworkManager", Section 22.1 "Use Cases for NetworkManager"*.

2.6 Exploring the Internet

The GNOME desktop includes Firefox, a Mozilla*-based Web browser. You can start it by clicking *Applications* › *Internet* › *Firefox*.

You can type an address into the location bar at the top or click links in a page to move to different pages, like in any other Web browser.

For more information, see *Chapter 16, Firefox: Browsing the Web*.

2.7   E-mail and Scheduling

For reading and managing your mail and events, use Evolution. Evolution is a groupware program that makes it easy to store, organize and retrieve your personal information.

Evolution seamlessly combines e-mail, a calendar, an address book, and a memo and task list in one easy-to-use application. With its extensive support for communications and data interchange standards, Evolution can work with existing corporate networks and applications, including Microsoft* Exchange.

To start Evolution, click *Applications > Internet > Evolution.*

The first time you start Evolution, it prompts you with a few questions to set up a mail account and import mail from an old mail client. Then it shows you how many new messages you have and lists upcoming appointments and tasks. The calendar, address book and mail tools are available in the shortcut bar on the left.

For more information, see *Chapter 12, Evolution: E-Mailing and Calendaring*.

2.8 Opening or Creating Documents with Libre-Office

For creating and editing documents, LibreOffice is installed with the GNOME desktop. LibreOffice is a complete set of office tools that can both read and save Microsoft Office file formats. LibreOffice has a word processor, a spreadsheet, a database, a drawing tool and a presentation program.

To start LibreOffice, click *Applications* › *Office* › *LibreOffice.*

For more information, see *Chapter 8, LibreOffice: The Office Suite.*

2.9 Controlling Your Desktop's Power Management

To see the state of the computer battery, check the battery icon in the right part of the panel. On certain events, such as a critically low battery state, GNOME will display notifications informing you about the event.

You can open the power settings via *Applications* › *System Tools* › *Settings* › *Power.*

For more information, see *Section 3.3.2, "Configuring Power Settings".*

2.10 Creating, Displaying, and Decompressing Archives

You can use the Archive Manager application (also known as File Roller) to create, view, modify or unpack an archive. An archive is a file that acts as a container for other files. An archive can contain many files, directories and subdirectories, usually in compressed form. Archive Manager supports common formats such as `zip`, `tar.gz`, `tar.bz2`, `lzh`, and `rar`. You can use Archive Manager to create, open and extract a compressed non-archive file.

To start Archive Manager, click *Applications* › *Utilities* › *Archive Manager.*

If you already have a compressed file, double-click the file name in GNOME Files to view the contents of the archive in Archive Manager.

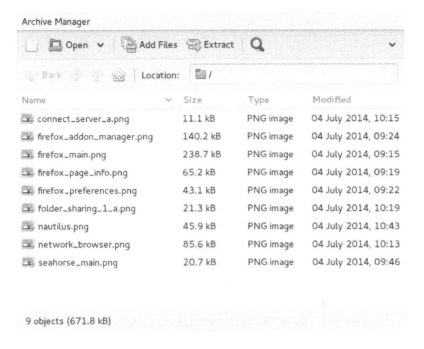

FIGURE 2.2: ARCHIVE MANAGER

2.10.1 Opening an Archive

1. In Archive Manager, click *Open*.

2. Select the archive you want to open.

3. Click *Open*.

   Archive Manager displays the following:

   - The archive name in the titlebar.

   - The archive contents in the content area.

   - The total number of files in the archive and the size of the archive when uncompressed, in the statusbar.

   To open another archive, click *Open* again. Archive Manager opens each archive in a new window. To open another archive in the same window, you must first select *Close* from the menu in the right part of the window to close the current archive, then click *Open*. If you try to open an archive that was created in a format that Archive Manager does not recognize, the application displays an error message.

2.10.2   Extracting Files from an Archive

1. In Archive Manager, select the files that you want to extract.

2. Click *Extract*.

3. Specify the directory where Archive Manager will extracts the files.

4. Choose from the following extraction options:

Option	Description
All files	Extracts all files from the archive.
Selected files	Extracts the selected files from the archive.
Files	Extracts from the archive all files that match the specified pattern.
Keep directory structure	Reconstructs the directory structure when extracting the specified files.
	For example, you specify `/tmp` in the *Filename* text box and extract all files. The archive contains a subdirectory called `doc`. If you select the *Keep directory structure* option, Archive Manager extracts the contents of the subdirectory to `/tmp/doc`.
	If you do not select the *Keep directory structure* option, Archive Manager does not create any subdirectories. Instead, it extracts all files from the archive, including files from subdirectories, to `/tmp`.
Do not overwrite newer files	If not active, the Archive Manager overwrites any files in the destination directory that have the same name as the specified files.
	If you select this option, Archive Manager does not extract the specified file if an existing file with the same name already exists in the destination directory.

5. Click *Extract*.

To extract an archived file in a file manager window without opening Archive Manager, right-click the file and select *Extract Here*.

The Extract operation extracts a copy of the specified files from the archive. The extracted files have the same permissions and modification date as the original files that were added to the archive.

The Extract operation does not change the contents of the archive.

2.10.3 Creating Archives

1. In Archive Manager, click the white icon in the top left part of the window.

2. Specify the name and location of the new archive.

3. Select an archive type from the drop-down box.

4. Click *Create*.
   Archive Manager creates an empty archive, but does not yet write the archive to disk. Archive Manager writes a new archive to disk only when the archive contains at least one file. If you create a new archive and quit Archive Manager before you add any files to the archive, the archive will be deleted.

5. Add files and directories to the new archive:

   a. Click *Add Files* and select the files or directories you want to add.

   b. Click *Add*.
      Archive Manager adds the files to the current directory in the archive.

You can also add files to an archive in a file manager window without opening Archive Manager. See *Section 2.1.2, "Compressing Files or Directories"* for more information.

2.11 Taking Screenshots

You can take a snapshot of your screen or of an individual application window by using the Take Screenshots utility. Start it by pressing `Print` to take a screenshot of the entire desktop or by pressing `Alt`-`Print` to take a screenshot of the currently active window or dialog.

The screenshots are automatically saved to your `~/Pictures` directory.

You can also use GIMP to take screenshots. In GIMP, click *File* › *Create* › *Screenshot*, select an area, choose a delay and then click *Snap*.

2.12   Viewing PDF Files

Documents that need to be shared or printed across platforms can be saved as PDF (Portable Document Format) files. Document Viewer (also known as Evince) can open PDF files and many similar file types, such as XPS, DjVu, or TIFF.

 Note: Rare Display Issues

In rare cases, documents will not be displayed correctly in Document Viewer. This can happen, for example, with certain forms, animations or 3D images. In such cases, ask the authors of the file what viewer they recommend. However, in at least some cases the recommended viewer will not work on Linux.

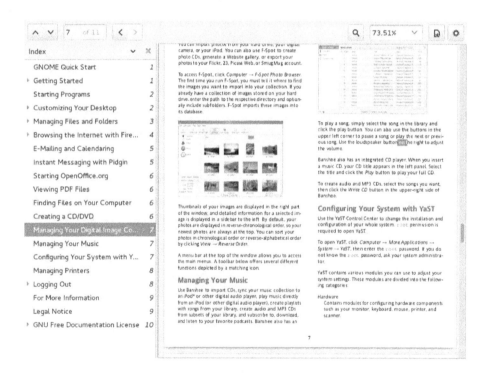

FIGURE 2.3: DOCUMENT VIEWER

To open Document Viewer, double-click a PDF file in a file manager window. Document Viewer will also open when you download a PDF file from a Web site. To open Document Viewer without a file, select *Applications › Office › Document Viewer.*

To view a PDF file in Document Viewer, click the cog wheel icon to open the menu and select *Open.* Now locate the desired PDF file and click *Open.*

Use the navigation icons at the top of the window or the thumbnails in the left panel to navigate through the document. If your PDF document provides bookmarks, you can access them in the left panel of the viewer.

2.13 Obtaining Software Updates

When you connect to the Internet, the updater applet automatically checks whether software updates for your system are available. When important updates are available, you will receive a notification on your desktop.

For detailed information on how to install software updates with the updater applet and how to configure it, refer to the chapter about installing and removing software in *Book "Deployment Guide", Chapter 5 "Installing or Removing Software", Section 5.4 "Keeping the System Up-to-date".*

2.14 For More Information

Along with the applications described in this chapter for getting started, you can use many other applications on GNOME. Find detailed information about these applications in the other parts of this manual.

To learn more about GNOME and GNOME applications, see http://www.gnome.org.

To report bugs or add feature requests, go to http://bugzilla.gnome.org.

3 Customizing Your Settings

You can change the way the GNOME desktop looks and behaves to suit your own personal tastes and needs. Some possible changes of settings are:

- Keyboard and mouse configuration, as described in *Section 3.3.3, "Modifying Keyboard Settings"* and *Section 3.3.4, "Configuring the Mouse and Touchpad"*

- Desktop background, as described in *Section 3.2.1, "Changing the Desktop Background and Lock Screen Appearance"*

- Sounds, as described in *Section 3.3.7, "Configuring Sound Settings"*

These settings and others can be changed in the *All Settings* dialog.

3.1 The GNOME Settings Dialog

YaST is a desktop-independent system-wide tool to configure most aspects of your SUSE Linux Enterprise Desktop installation. For example, it lets you configure hardware settings, network devices and services, software management or virtualization. The settings dialog is a GNOME configuration tool and focuses on look and feel, personal settings and preferences of your GNOME desktop.

To access the settings dialog, click *Applications* › *System Tools* › *Settings*. The dialog is divided into the following three categories:

Personal

Go here to change your login password, language settings and keyboard layout. You can also modify the desktop background or set up accounts for e-mail, chat and cloud providers. For more information, see *Section 3.2, "Personal"*.

Hardware

Allows you to configure hardware components such as monitors, printers, mouses/touchpads, network adapters and sound devices. You can also change key combination settings and set up power-saving features. For more information, see *Section 3.3, "Hardware"*.

System

> Lets you configure system settings such as date and time, whether to start software when inserting USB drives or whether you want to share your screen with others. You can also set up user accounts. If you want, you can also start YaST from this screen, though it is also available separately from within the menu. For more information, see *Section 3.4, "System"*.

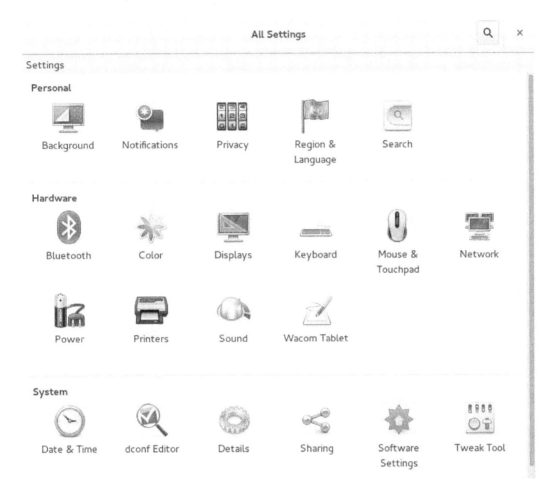

To change some system-wide settings, the control center will prompt you for the root password and start YaST. This is mostly the case for administrator settings (including most of the hardware, the graphical user interface, Internet access, security settings, user administration, software installation and system updates and information). Follow the instructions in YaST to configure these settings. For information about using YaST, refer to the integrated YaST help texts or to the *Book* "Deployment Guide".

This chapter focuses on individual settings you can change directly in the GNOME settings dialog, without having to use YaST.

3.2 Personal

The following sections introduce examples of how to configure some personal aspects of your GNOME desktop, like your languages used or desktop backgrounds.

3.2.1 Changing the Desktop Background and Lock Screen Appearance

The desktop background is the image or color that is applied to your desktop. You can also customize the image shown when the screen is locked.

To change the desktop background or the lock screen:

1. Click *Applications* › *System Tools* › *Settings* › *Background*.

2. Click *Background* or *Lock Screen*.

3. Click *Wallpapers*, *Pictures*, or *Colors*.
   Wallpapers are preconfigured images distributed with your system. Pictures are your own images from your `Pictures` directory (`~/Pictures`). Colors are predefined colors chosen by GNOME developers.

4. Choose an option from the list.

5. When you are satisfied with your choice, click *Select*.

3.2.2 Configuring Language Settings

SUSE Linux Enterprise Desktop can be configured to use any of several languages. The language setting determines the language of dialogs and menus and can also determine the keyboard and clock layout.

To configure your language settings click *Applications* › *System Tools* › *Settings* › *Region and Language*.

Here you can choose:

- Interface language

- Date and number formats, currency and related options

- Input sources (for many languages that means keyboard layouts only, though for non-alphabetic languages there can be additional settings)

3.3 Hardware

In the following sections you will find examples of how to configure some hardware aspects of your GNOME desktop, including keyboard or mouse preferences, handling of removable drives (and other media) or screen resolution.

3.3.1 Configuring Bluetooth Settings

The Bluetooth module lets you set the visibility of your machine over Bluetooth and connect to available Bluetooth devices. To configure Bluetooth connectivity, follow these steps:

1. Click *Applications* › *System Tools* › *Settings* › *Bluetooth* to open the Bluetooth settings module.

2. To use Bluetooth, turn the *Bluetooth* switch on.

3. To make your computer visible over Bluetooth, turn the *Visibility* switch on. You do not need this option to be turned on to connect to a Bluetooth device after the initial setup.

    Note: Temporary Visibility

   Visibility is only meant to be used temporarily. You do not need this option to be turned on to connect to a Bluetooth device after the initial setup.

   However, on SUSE Linux Enterprise Desktop, the *Visibility* setting will not automatically be turned off after a certain period of time. Instead, you will need to turn it off yourself.

4. The *Devices* list contains all known Bluetooth devices. At first, it may be empty.

To add a device to the list, click the plus icon in the lower left corner.

5. On the device you want to connect, turn on Bluetooth connectivity and visibility.

6. Select the desired device from the list.
   To filter for a specific device, open the drop-down box next to *Device Type* and choose a type such as *Phone*. To see all available devices, use *All Types*.
   To change whether to use a PIN, click *PIN Options*. Then select the appropriate option. However, usually you do not need to change PIN options.

7. Click *Continue*. You will now need to wait for a few seconds.

8. If a PIN was used, confirm whether the PIN of the two devices matched. You need to do this on both devices. The device should now be connected.
   Depending on the device type, you can now either see it as a storage device in GNOME Files, set a volume for it in the Sound settings or other things.

To remove a device from the list, select the device and click the minus icon.

To connect to a Bluetooth device, select the device in the list and turn the *Connection* switch on. You can send files to the connected device using the *Send Files* button. If you are connected to a device such as a mobile phone, you can use it as a network device by activating the appropriate option.

3.3.2   Configuring Power Settings

1. Click *Applications* › *System Tools* › *Settings* › *Power* to open the Power settings module.

2. In the upper part of the dialog, you can see the current state of the battery.

3. In the *Power Saving* section of the dialog, set the *Screen Brightness* to conserve power. You can also set whether to dim the screen after a period of inactivity and set the time interval. You can also set whether to turn off wireless networking after the period of inactivity.

4. In the *Suspend and Power Off* section of the dialog, set the *Automatic Suspend*. When you click it, a separate dialog opens.
   In it, you can turn on automatic suspending and associated time intervals. If you are using a computer with a battery, you can set these separately for computer running on battery power or plugged in.

You can also set the action performed when the battery power is critical. Choose *Hibernation* to use a mode where the computer turns off completely but saves your running session to the hard disk. Alternatively, choose *Power Off* to turn the computer off without saving the session.

3.3.3 Modifying Keyboard Settings

To modify keyboard settings (such as key autorepetition and the cursor blink rate), click *Applications > System Tools > Settings > Keyboard.*

FIGURE 3.2: KEYBOARD SETTINGS DIALOG

- On the *Typing* tab, you can set some general keyboard preferences, such as enabling keyboard repeat with individual delay and speed options or enabling or disabling the blinking of the cursor and defining the speed.

- On the *Shortcuts* tab, you can set key combinations for the desktop.
  To edit a key combination, first click the row. To set a new key combination, hold it down. To disable a shortcut, press ⟵ instead.

To configure keyboard accessibility options, refer to *Section 4.4, "Mobility Impairments"*. To configure your keyboard layout, refer to *Section 3.2.2, "Configuring Language Settings"*.

3.3.4 Configuring the Mouse and Touchpad

To modify mouse and touchpad options, click *Applications > System Tools > Settings > Mouse and Touchpad.*

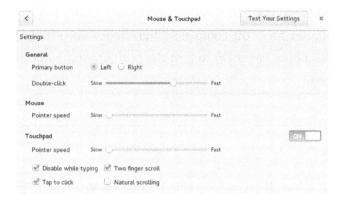

FIGURE 3.3: MOUSE AND TOUCHPAD SETTINGS DIALOG

- In the *General* section of the dialog, you can set the *Primary button* orientation (left or right) and the speed of the double-click.

- In the *Mouse* section of the dialog, use *Pointer Speed* to adjust the sensitivity of the mouse pointer.

- In the *Touchpad* section of the dialog, you can turn the touchpad on and off. Use *Pointer Speed* to adjust the sensitivity of the touchpad pointer. You can also disable the touchpad while typing and enable clicks by tapping the touchpad.

- To test your settings, click *Test Your Settings* and try the pointing device. Click *Done* when you are finished.

For configuration of mouse accessibility options, refer to the *Section 4.4, "Mobility Impairments"*.

3.3.5   Installing and Configuring Printers

The *Printers* module lets you connect to any available local or remote CUPS server and configure printers.

To start the Printers module, click *Applications › System Tools › Settings › Printers*. For detailed information, refer to *Chapter 6, Managing Printers*.

3.3.6   Configuring Screens

To specify resolution and orientation for your screen or to configure multiple screens, click *Applications › System Tools › Settings › Displays*.

1. To find the right monitor, look for the numbers displayed in the upper left corner of all monitors. To set options for a monitor, click the list item of the monitor. A new dialog appears.

2. If multiple monitors are attached to the computer, the left part of the dialog will allow you to choose how to use the monitor. You can choose between:

   Primary

   > The screen that shows the panel and important messages.

   Secondary Display

   > A monitor that expands the desktop of the primary monitor.

   Mirror

   > A monitor that mirrors the image on the primary monitor. In terms of resolution, the lowest common denominator will be used.

   Turn Off

   > A screen that is not used.

   To rotate the displayed image, use the buttons with the arrows pointing left and right. To mirror the displayed image, use the button with the double arrow icon.

   You can set a different resolution by changing the value next to *Resolution*. Not all resolutions provide a sharp and unstretched image. To find the best resolution for your monitor, refer to its manual.

3. When you are done, click *Apply*.

   The monitors will now readjust. This can take multiple seconds during which the screen can be black or distorted.

   Afterwards, a confirmation dialog will appear.

4. If the configuration looks correct, click *Keep Changes*.

   If the configuration is not what you hoped for, click *Revert Settings* or wait for 20 seconds. The changes will then be reverted.

FIGURE 3.4: MONITOR RESOLUTION SETTINGS DIALOG

PROCEDURE 3.2: CHANGING THE ARRANGEMENT OF MULTIPLE MONITORS

If you are using multiple screens, set up how they are arranged, so you can use the mouse pointer properly across monitors.

1. Click *Arrange Combined Displays*.

2. To find the right monitor, look for the numbers displayed in the upper left corner of all monitors. Click and drag a monitor around to move it.

3. When you are done, click *Apply*.

4. If the configuration looks correct, click *Keep Changes*.
   If the configuration is not what you hoped for, click *Revert Settings* or wait for 20 seconds. The changes will then be reverted.

3.3.7 Configuring Sound Settings

The *Sound* tool lets you manage sound devices and set the sound effects. In the top part of the dialog, you can select the general output volume or turn the sound off completely.

To open the sound settings, click *Applications* › *System Tools* › *Settings* › *Sound*.

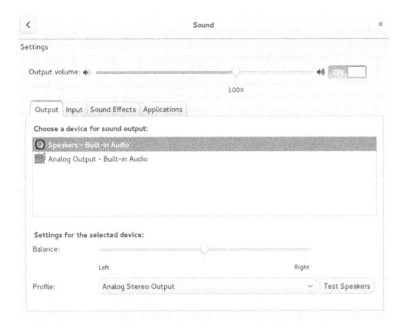

FIGURE 3.5: CONFIGURING SOUND SETTINGS

3.3.7.1 Configuring Sound Devices

Use the *Output* tab to select the device for sound output. Below the list, choose the sound device setting you prefer, for example balance.

Use the *Input* tab to set the input device volume or to mute the input temporarily. If you have more than one sound device, you can also select a default device for audio input in the *Choose a device for sound input* list.

3.3.7.2 Configuring Sound Effects

Use the *Sound Effects* tab to configure whether and how you want sound to be played when message boxes appear.

Specify the volume at which the sound effects will be played under *Alert volume*. You can also turn the effects on and off.

Select the *Alert Sound* to use.

3.3.8 Networking

To set up networking options, click *Applications > System Tools > Settings > Network*.

In the appearing dialog, you can configure wired or wireless connections and proxies and VPNs. If you are unsure which network parameters to use, refer to your system administrator.

To learn more about setting up network connections, see *Book "Administration Guide", Chapter 22 "Using NetworkManager"*.

3.4 System

In the following sections, you will find examples of how to configure some system aspects of your GNOME desktop. These include preferred applications, changing your user password, and session sharing preferences.

To learn more about configuring assistive technologies, see *Chapter 4, Assistive Technologies*.

3.4.1 Changing Your Password

For security reasons, it is a good idea to change your login password from time to time. To change your password:

1. Click *Applications > System Tools > Settings > Users*.

2. Click the button labeled with dots next to *Password*.

3. In the first text box, type your current password.

4. In the next text box, type a new password.
   You can also click the cog wheel icon at the end of the text box to generate a random password.

5. Confirm your new password by typing it again in the last text box.

6. Then click *Change*.

3.4.2 Setting Preferred Applications

The Preferred Applications module allows you to change the default application for various common tasks such as browsing the Internet, sending mails or playing multimedia files.

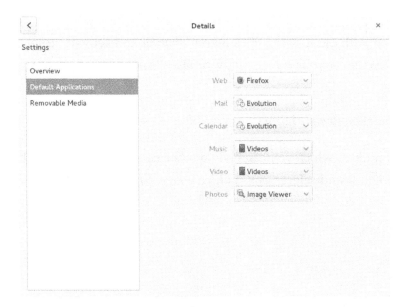

FIGURE 3.6: PREFERRED APPLICATIONS

1. Click *Applications* > *System Tools* > *Settings* > *Details*.

2. Click *Default Applications*.

3. Select one of the available applications from the drop-down box. You can choose an application to handle Web, mail, calendar, music, videos or photographs.

3.4.3 Setting Session Sharing Preferences

The *Remote Desktop Preference* dialog lets you share a GNOME desktop session between multiple users and set session-sharing preferences.

> **Important: Sharing Desktop Sessions Affects System Security**
> Sharing desktop sessions can be a security risk. Use the restriction options available.

Click *Applications* > *System Tools* > *Settings* > *Sharing*.

Before you can share anything, you need to turn on the switch in the upper part of the dialog. It can also help you if you quickly need to disable all sharing options.

- To share your public directory over the network, click *Personal File Sharing* and turn on *Share Public Folder On This Network*. You can also set a password.

- To share your desktop session with other users, click *Screen Sharing* and activate *Remote View*. To allow other users to control your screen, activate also *Remote Control*. You can also set a password.

- To enable logging in via SSH, click *Remote Login*.

All the sharing screens contain an address which you can give to other users, so they can reach you. To copy a sharing address, click it and select *Copy*. You can then paste it into an e-mail or messaging software.

3.4.4   Setting Software Updates

The *Software Updates* tool lets you configure the frequency of update checking and which sources you want to receive updates from.

Click *Applications* › *System Tools* › *Settings* › *Software Settings*.

For more information, see *Book "Deployment Guide", Chapter 5 "Installing or Removing Software", Section 5.4.3 "Configuring the GNOME Software Updater".*

3.4.5   Configuring Administrative Settings with YaST

For your convenience, YaST is available from the Control Panel as well as the Applications menu. For information about using YaST, refer to *Book "Deployment Guide".*

4 Assistive Technologies

The GNOME desktop includes assistive technologies to support users with various impairments and special needs, and to interact with common assistive devices. This chapter describes several assistive technology applications designed to meet the needs of users with physical disabilities like low vision or impaired motor skills.

4.1 Enabling Assistive Technologies

To configure accessibility features, open the GNOME Settings dialog (for example using *Applications* › *System Tools* › *Settings*) and click *Universal Access*. Each assistive feature is enabled separately using this dialog.

If you need a more direct access to individual assistive features, check *Always Show Universal Access Menu* in the *Universal Access* dialog. A new menu will appear on the bottom panel.

4.2 Visual Impairments

In the *Seeing* section of the *Universal Access* dialog, you can enable features that help people with impaired vision.

- Turning on *High Contrast* enables high contrast black and white icons in the GNOME desktop.

- Turning on *Large Text* enlarges the font used in the user interface.

- Turning on *Zoom* enables a screen magnifier. You can set the desired magnification and magnifier behavior, including color effects.

- If the *Screen Reader* is turned on, any UI element or text that receives keyboard focus is read aloud.

- If the *Sound Keys* are turned on, a sound is played whenever `Num Lock` or `Caps Lock` are turned on.

4.3 Hearing Impairments

In the *Hearing* section of the *Universal Access* dialog, you can enable features helping people with impaired hearing.

If the *Visual Alerts* are turned on, a window title or the entire screen is flashed when an alert sound occurs.

4.4 Mobility Impairments

In the *Typing* and *Pointing and Clicking* sections of the *Universal Access* dialog, you can enable features that help people with mobility impairments.

- If the *Screen Keyboard* is turned on, a virtual keyboard appears whenever you need to enter text. You can use the screen keyboard by clicking the virtual keys.

- Click *Typing Assist* to open a dialog where you can enable various features that make typing easier.

  - *Sticky Keys* allows you to type key combinations one key at a time rather than having to hold down all of the keys at once. For example, the `Alt`-`→|` shortcut switches between windows.
  With sticky keys turned off, you need to hold down both keys at the same time. With sticky keys turned on, press `Alt` and then `→|` to do the same.

  - Turn on *Slow Keys* if you want a delay between pressing a key and the letter being displayed on the screen. This means that you need to hold down each key you want to type for a little while before it appears. Use slow keys if you accidentally press several keys at a time when you type, or if you find it difficult to press the right key on the keyboard first time.

  - Turn on *Bounce Keys* to ignore key presses that are rapidly repeated. This can help, for example, if you have hand tremors which cause you to press a key multiple times when you only want to press it once.

  - Turn on *Mouse Keys* to control the mouse pointer using the numeric keypad on your keyboard.

- Click *Click Assist* to open a dialog where you can enable various features that make clicking easier: simulated secondary click and hover click.

- Turn on *Simulated Secondary Click* to activate the secondary click (usually the right mouse button) by holding down the primary button for a predefined *Acceptance delay*. This is useful if you find it difficult to move your fingers individually on one hand, or if your pointing device only has a single button.

- Turn on *Hover Click* to trigger a click by hovering your mouse pointer over an object on the screen. This is useful if you find it difficult to move the mouse and click at the same time. If this feature is turned on, a small Hover Click window opens and stays above all of your other windows. You can use this to choose what sort of click should happen when you hover. When you hover your mouse pointer over a button and do not move it, the pointer gradually changes color. When it has fully changed color, the button will be clicked.

4.5 For More Information

You can find further information in the GNOME help, which is also available online at https://help.gnome.org/users/gnome-help/3.12/a11y.html.en.

II Connectivity, Files and Resources

5 Accessing Network Resources

From your desktop, you can access files and directories or certain services on remote hosts or make your own files and directories available to other users in your network. SUSE® Linux Enterprise Desktop offers the following ways of accessing and creating network shared resources.

Network Browsing

Your file manager, GNOME Files, lets you browse your network for shared resources and services. Learn more about this in *Section 5.3, "Accessing Network Shares"*.

Sharing Directories in Mixed Environments

Using GNOME Files, configure your files and directories to share with other members of your network. Make your data readable or writable for users from any Windows or Linux workstation. Learn more about this in *Section 5.4, "Sharing Directories"*.

Managing Windows Files

SUSE Linux Enterprise Desktop can be configured to integrate into an existing Windows network. Your Linux machine then behaves like a Windows client. It takes all account information from the Active Directory domain controller, just as the Windows clients do. Learn more about this in *Section 5.5, "Managing Windows Files"*.

Configuring and Accessing a Windows Network Printer

You can configure a Windows network printer through the GNOME control center. Learn how to do this in *Section 5.6, "Configuring and Accessing a Windows Network Printer"*.

5.1 Connecting to a Network

You can connect to a network with wired and wireless connections. To view your network connection, check the icon in the right part of the main panel. If you click the icon, you can see more details in the menu. Click the connection name to see more details and access the settings.

To learn more about connecting to a network, see *Book* "Administration Guide", *Chapter 22* "*Using NetworkManager*".

5.2 General Notes on File Sharing and Network Browsing

 Important: Contact Your Administrator Before Setup

Whether and to what extent you can use file sharing and network browsing and in your network highly depends on the network structure and on the configuration of your machine.

Before setting up either of them, contact your system administrator. Check whether your network structure supports a feature and whether your company's security policies permit it.

Network browsing, be it SMB browsing for Windows shares or SLP browsing for remote services, relies heavily on the machine's ability to send broadcast messages to all clients in the network. These messages and the clients' replies to them enable your machine to detect any available shares or services.

For broadcasts to work effectively, your machine must be part of the same subnet as all other machines it is querying. If network browsing does not work on your machine or the detected shares and services do not meet your expectations, contact your system administrator to ensure that you are connected to the appropriate subnet.

To allow network browsing, your machine needs to keep several network ports open to send and receive network messages that provide details on the network and the availability of shares and services. The standard SUSE Linux Enterprise Desktop is configured for tight security and has a firewall that protects your machine against the Internet.

To adjust the firewall configuration, you would either need to ask your system administrator to put your interface into the internal zone or to tear down the firewall entirely (depending on your company's security policy). If you try to browse a network with a restrictive firewall running on your machine, GNOME Files warns you that your security restrictions are not allowing it to query the network.

5.3 Accessing Network Shares

Networking workstations can be set up to share directories. Typically, files and directories are marked to allow users remote access. These are called *network shares*. If your system is configured to access network shares, you can use your file manager to access these shares and browse them just as easily as if they were located on your local machine. Your level of access to the shared directories (whether read-only or write access, as well) is dependent on the permissions granted to you by the owner of the shares.

To access network shares, open GNOME Files and click *Browse Network* from the *Places* pane. GNOME Files displays the servers and networks that you can access. Double-click a server or network to access its shares. You might be required to authenticate to the server by providing a user name and password. Common network shares are SFTP-accessible resources (SSH File Transfer Protocol) or Windows shares.

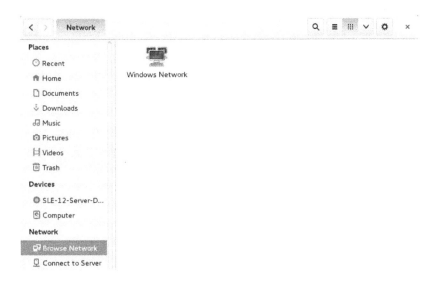

FIGURE 5.1: NETWORK FILE BROWSER

PROCEDURE 5.1: ADDING A NETWORK PLACE

1. Click *Applications* › *Accessories* › *Files* › *Connect to Server*.

Server Address

For example, smb://foo.example.org

Recent Servers

Browse   Cancel   Connect

FIGURE 5.2: CONNECT TO THE SERVER DIALOG

2. Enter the server address.

3. Click *Connect*.

5.4 Sharing Directories

Sharing and exchanging documents is a must-have in corporate environments. GNOME Files offers you file sharing, which makes your files and directories available to both Linux and Windows users.

5.4.1 Enabling Sharing on the Computer

Before you can share a directory, you must enable sharing on your computer. To enable sharing:

1. Start YaST from the main menu.

2. Enter the `root` password.

3. In the category *Network Services*, click *Windows Domain Membership*.

4. Click *Allow Users to Share Their Directories*, then click *OK*.

5.4.2   Enabling Sharing for a Directory

To configure file sharing for a directory:

1. Open GNOME Files.

2. Right-click a directory, then select *Sharing Options* from the context menu.

3. Select *Share this folder.*

4. If you want other people to be able to write to the directory, select *Allow other people to write in this folder.* To allow access for people without a user account check *Guest Access.*

5. Click *Create Share.*

6. If the directory does not already have the permissions that are required for sharing, a dialog appears. Click *Add the permissions automatically.*

The directory icon changes to indicate that the directory is now shared.

> **❗ Important: Samba Domain Browsing and Firewalls**
>
> Samba domain browsing only works if your system's firewall is configured accordingly. Either disable the firewall entirely or assign the browsing interface to the internal firewall zone. Ask your system administrator how to proceed.

5.5 Managing Windows Files

With your SUSE Linux Enterprise Desktop machine being an Active Directory client, you can browse, view and manipulate data located on Windows servers. The following examples are the most prominent ones:

Browsing Windows Files with GNOME Files

Use GNOME Files's network browsing features to browse your Windows data.

Viewing Windows Data with GNOME Files

Use GNOME Files to display the contents of your Windows user directory as you would for displaying a Linux directory. Create new files and directories on the Windows server.

Manipulating Windows Data with GNOME Applications

Many GNOME applications allow you to open files on the Windows server, manipulate them and save them back to the Windows server.

Single Sign-On

GNOME applications, including GNOME Files, support Single Sign-On. This means that you do not need to re-authenticate when you access other Windows resources. These can be Web servers, proxy servers or groupware servers like Microsoft Exchange*. Authentication against all these is handled silently in the background using the user name and password you provided when you logged in.

To access your Windows data using GNOME Files, proceed as follows:

1. Open GNOME Files and click *Network* in the Places pane.

2. Double-click *Windows Network*.

3. Double-click the icon of the workgroup containing the computer you want to access.

4. Click the computer's icon (and authenticate if prompted to do so) and navigate to the shared directory on that computer.

To create directories in your Windows user directory using GNOME Files, proceed as you would when creating a Linux directory.

5.6 Configuring and Accessing a Windows Network Printer

Being part of a corporate network and authenticating against a Windows Active Directory server, you can access corporate resources such as printers. GNOME allows you to configure printing from your Linux client to a Windows network printer.

To configure a Windows network printer for use through your Linux workstation, proceed as follows:

1. Start the GNOME control center from the main menu by clicking *Applications* › *System Tools* › *Settings* › *Printers*.

2. Click *Unlock* and enter the `root` password.

3. Click the plus icon.

4. Select a Windows printer connected via Samba.

To print to the Windows network printer configured above, select it from the list of available printers.

6 Managing Printers

SUSE® Linux Enterprise Desktop makes it easy to print your documents, whether your computer is connected directly to a printer or linked remotely on a network. This chapter describes how to set up printers in SUSE Linux Enterprise Desktop and manage print jobs.

6.1 Installing a Printer

Before you can install a printer, you need to know the `root` password and have your printer information ready. Depending on how you connect the printer, you might also need the printer URI, TCP/IP address or host, and the driver for the printer. A number of common printer drivers ship with SUSE Linux Enterprise Desktop. If you cannot find a driver for the printer, check the printer manufacturer's Web site.

1. Click *Applications* > *System Tools* > *Settings* > *Printers*.

2. Click *Unlock* and enter the root password.

3. Click the plus icon.

4. If there are too many printers in the list, filter them by entering an IP address or a keyword into the search field in the lower part of the dialog.

5. Select a printer from the list of available printers and click *Add*.

The installed printer appears in the Printers panel. You can now print to the printer from any application.

7 Backing Up User Data

The Backup tool is a simple framework to let users back up and restore their own data such as home directories or selected files. It is possible to create scheduled backups or backups on request, and to play back a previous state of this data.

7.1 Creating Backups

First schedule which data you want to back up and when to do it.

1. *Applications* › *System Tools* › *Backup*.

2. If you are opening the application for the first time, you will see a screen welcoming you. Click *Just Show My Settings*.

3. On the *Overview* tab you can turn the *Automatic backups* on and off. You can also see the overview of the current settings.

4. On the *Exceptions* tab add files and directories you want to exclude from the backup.

5. On the *Folders* tab select the directories to back up and directories to ignore. For example, if you want to back up your home directory except for the `Downloads` directory, add your home directory to back up and your `Downloads` directory to ignore.

6. On the *Schedule* tab select how often to perform the automatic backups (daily or weekly) and how long to keep the backups.

7. If you want to perform a backup immediately, too, click *Back Up Now*.

    a. Choose whether you want the backup to be password-protected.
    If so, type a password in the two text boxes next to *Encryption Password* and *Confirm Password*.
    If not, click *Allow Restoring Without a Password*.

    b. Click *Continue*. The backup process will now start. When the backup is finished, the window will close.

7.2 Restoring Data

To restore a previous state of your data, proceed as follows:

1. Select *Applications* › *System Tools* › *Backup*.

2. On the *Overview* tab, click *Restore*.

3. Choose the location from which to restore. Click *Forward*.

4. Choose a date. Click *Forward*.

5. Choose where to restore. Click *Restore*.

III LibreOffice

8 LibreOffice: The Office Suite

LibreOffice is an open source office suite that provides tools for all types of office tasks such as writing texts, working with spreadsheets, or creating graphics and presentations. With LibreOffice, you can use the same data across different computing platforms. You can also open and edit files in other formats, including Microsoft Office, then save them back to this format, if needed. This chapter contains information that applies to all of the LibreOffice modules.

8.1 LibreOffice Modules

LibreOffice consists of several application modules (subprograms), which are designed to interact with each other. They are listed in *Table 8.1*. A full description of each module is available in the online help, described in *Section 8.10, "For More Information"*.

TABLE 8.1: THE LIBREOFFICE APPLICATION MODULES

Module	Purpose
Writer	Word processor application module
Calc	Spreadsheet application module
Impress	Presentation application module
Base	Database application module
Draw	Application module for drawing vector graphics
Math	Application module for generating mathematical formulas

8.2 Starting LibreOffice

To start LibreOffice click *Applications* > *Office* > *LibreOffice.*

The following chapters cover individual LibreOffice modules:

Chapter 9, LibreOffice Writer

Introduces LibreOffice Writer.

Introduces LibreOffice Calc.

Introduces LibreOffice Impress, Base, Draw, and Math.

In the selection dialog, choose the module you want to open or which file type you want to create. If any LibreOffice application is open, you can start any of the other applications by clicking *File > New > Name of Application.*

You can also start individual LibreOffice modules from your main menu. As an alternative, use the command **libreoffice** and one of the options `--writer`, `--calc`, `--impress`, `--draw` or `--base` to start the respective module. Find more useful options with `--help`.

Before you start working with LibreOffice, you may be interested in changing some options from the preferences dialog. Click *Tools > Options* to open it. The most important ones are:

LibreOffice > User Data

Insert your user data like company, first and last name, street, city, and other useful information. This data is used in LibreOffice Writer for annotations, for example.

LibreOffice > Fonts

Offers mappings from one font name to another. This could be useful, if you exchange documents with others and the document you received contains fonts that are not available on your system.

Load/Save > General

Contains loading and saving specific options. For example, you can choose whether to always create a backup copy and which default file format LibreOffice should use.

To learn more about configuring LibreOffice, see *Section 8.7, "Changing the Global Settings".*

8.3 Compatibility with Other Office Applications

LibreOffice can work with documents, spreadsheets, presentations, and databases in many other formats, including Microsoft Office. They can be easily opened like other files and saved back to the original format. If you have problems with your documents, consider opening them in the original application and resaving them in an open format such as RTF for text documents.

In case of migration issues with spreadsheets, however, it is advisable to always save them as Excel files. Use the Excel format as an intermediate format. The CSV format can work, too, but you will lose all cell formatting. CSV sometimes also leads to incorrect cell type detection for spreadsheets.

8.3.1 Converting Documents to the LibreOffice Format

LibreOffice can read, edit, and save documents in several formats. It is not necessary to convert files from those formats to the LibreOffice format to use those files. However, if you want to convert the files, you can do so. To convert several documents, such as when first switching to LibreOffice, do the following:

1. Select *File > Wizards > Document Converter*.

2. Choose the file format from which to convert.

3. Click *Next*.

4. Specify where LibreOffice should look for templates and documents to convert and in which directory the converted files should be placed.
   Documents retrieved from a Windows partition are usually in a subdirectory of `/windows`.

5. Make sure that all other settings are correct, then click *Next*.

6. Review the summary of the actions to perform, then start the conversion by clicking *Convert*. When everything is done, close the Wizard by clicking *Close*.
   The amount of time needed for the conversion depends on the number of files and their complexity. For most documents, conversion does not take very long.

8.3.2 Sharing Files with Users of Other Office Suites

LibreOffice is available for several operating systems. This makes it an excellent tool when a group of users frequently need to share files and do not use the same system on their computers. When sharing documents with others, you have several options.

If the recipient needs to be able to edit the file

> Save the document in the format the other user needs. For example, to save as a Microsoft Word file, click *File › Save As*, then select the Microsoft Word file type for the version of Word the other user needs.

If the recipient only needs to read the document

> Export the document to a PDF file with *File › Export as PDF*. PDF files can be read on any platform using a PDF viewer.

If you want to share a document for editing

> Agree on a common exchange format that works for everyone. TXT and RTF formats, although limited in formatting, can be a good option for text documents.

If you want to e-mail a document as a PDF

> Click *File › Send › E-mail as PDF*. Your default e-mail program opens with the file attached.

If you want to e-mail a document to a Microsoft Word user

> Click *File › Send › E-mail as Microsoft Word*. Your default e-mail program opens with the file attached.

Send a document as the body of an e-mail

> Click *File › Send › Document as E-mail*. Your default e-mail program opens with the contents of the document as the e-mail body.

8.4 Saving LibreOffice Files with a Password

You can save files, no matter in which LibreOffice format, with a password. Note that this offers limited protection only. For stronger protection, use encryption methods as described in *Book "Security Guide", Chapter 11 "Encrypting Partitions and Files"*. To save a file with a password, select *File › Save* or *File › Save As*. In the dialog that opens, activate the *Save with password* check box and click *OK*. After you have typed and confirmed your password, your file will be saved. The next time a user opens the file, he will be prompted for the password.

To change the password, either overwrite the same file by selecting *File › Save As* or select *File › Properties* and click *Change Password* to access the password dialog.

8.5 Signing Documents

You can digitally sign documents to protect them. For this you need a personal certificate, similar to an HTTPS certificate. You can either create a self-signed certificate or choose to get one from a Certificate Authority.

When applying a digital signature to a document, a kind of checksum is created from the document's content and your personal key. The checksum is stored together with the document.

When another person opens the document, the checksum will be generated again. The new checksum is then compared to the original checksum If both are equal, the application will signal that the document has not been changed in the meantime.

To add a certificate to LibreOffice, you need to use Firefox. Start Firefox by selecting *Applications* › *Internet* › *Firefox*. Go to the certificates preferences by opening the menu (the button with the three-lines icon), then select *Preferences* › *Advanced* › *Certificates* › *View Certificates*. Add your certificate by selecting *Your Certificates* and clicking *Import* and then locate your certificate.

To sign a document, first open it in LibreOffice. Then select *File* › *Digital Signatures* › *Sign Document*. Select the certificate you want to use for signing, then click *OK*.

SUSE Linux Enterprise Desktop allows you to access certificates from the certificate store. For more information, refer to *Book "Security Guide", Chapter 12 "Certificate Store"*.

8.6 Customizing LibreOffice

You can customize LibreOffice to best suit your needs and working style. Toolbars, menus, and key combinations can all be reconfigured to help you more quickly access the features you use the most. You can also assign macros to application events if you want specific actions to occur when those events take place. For example, if you always work with a specific spreadsheet, you can create a macro that opens the spreadsheet and assign the macro to the Start Application event.

This section contains simple, generic instructions for customizing your environment. The changes you make are effective immediately, so you can see if the changes are what you wanted and go back and modify them if they are not. See the LibreOffice help files for detailed instructions.

To access the customization dialog in any open LibreOffice module, select *Tools* › *Customize*.

FIGURE 8.1: CUSTOMIZATION DIALOG IN WRITER

 Note: Further Information

Click *Help* for more information about the options in the *Customize* dialog.

PROCEDURE 8.1: CUSTOMIZING TOOLBARS

1. In the customization dialog, click the *Toolbar* tab.

2. From the *Toolbar* drop-down box, select the toolbar you want to customize.

3. Select the check boxes next to the commands you want to appear on the toolbar, and deselect the check boxes next to the commands you do not want to appear. A short description for each command is shown at the bottom of the dialog.

4. With *Save In*, select whether to save your customized toolbar in the current LibreOffice module or in the current document. If you decide to save it in the LibreOffice module, the customized toolbar is used whenever you open that module. If you decide to save it together with the current document, the customized toolbar is used whenever you open that document.

5. Repeat to customize additional toolbars.

6. Click *OK*.

If you want to switch back to the original settings again, open the customization dialog, click the *Toolbar* drop-down box and select *Restore Default Settings*. Click *Yes* and *Reset* to proceed.

PROCEDURE 8.2: SHOWING OR HIDING BUTTONS IN THE TOOLBAR

1. Click the arrow icon at the right edge of the toolbar you want to change.

2. Click *Visible Buttons* to display a list of buttons.

3. Select the buttons in the list to enable (check) or disable (uncheck) them.

PROCEDURE 8.3: CUSTOMIZING MENUS

You can add or delete items from current menus, reorganize menus, and even create new menus.

1. Click *Tools* › *Customize* › *Menus*.

2. Select the menu you want to change, or click *New* to create a new menu.

3. Modify, add, or delete menu items as desired.

4. Click *OK*.

PROCEDURE 8.4: CUSTOMIZING KEY COMBINATIONS

You can reassign currently assigned key combinations and assign new ones to frequently used functions.

1. Click *Tools* › *Customize* › *Keyboard*.

2. Select the keys you want to assign to a combination.

3. Select a *Category* and an appropriate *function*.

4. Click *Modify* to assign the function to the key or *Delete* to remove an existing assignment.

5. Click *OK*.

PROCEDURE 8.5: CUSTOMIZING EVENTS

LibreOffice also provides ways to assign macros to events such as application start-up or the saving of a document. The assigned macro runs automatically whenever the selected event occurs.

1. Click *Tools* › *Customize* › *Events*.

2. Select the event you want to change.

3. Assign or remove macros for the selected event.

4. Click *OK*.

8.7   Changing the Global Settings

Global settings can be changed in any LibreOffice application by clicking *Tools* › *Options* on the menu bar. This opens the window shown in the figure below. A tree structure is used to display categories of settings.

The settings categories that appear depend on the module you are working in. For example, if you are in Writer, the LibreOffice Writer category appears in the list, but the LibreOffice Calc category does not. The LibreOffice Base category appears in both Calc and Writer. The Module column in the table shows where each setting category is available.

The following table lists the settings categories along with a brief description of each category:

TABLE 8.2: GLOBAL SETTING CATEGORIES

Settings Category	Description	Module
LibreOffice	Various basic settings, including your user data (such as your address and e-mail), important paths, and settings for printers and external programs.	All

Settings Category	Description	Module
Load/Save	Includes the settings related to the opening and saving of several file types. There is a dialog for general settings and several special dialogs to define how external formats should be handled.	All
Language Settings	Covers the various settings related to languages and writing aids, such as your locale and spell checker settings. This is also the place to enable support for Asian languages.	All
LibreOffice Writer	Configures the global word processing options, such as the basic fonts and layout that Writer should use.	Writer
LibreOffice Writer/ Web	Changes the settings related to the HTML authoring features of LibreOffice.	Writer
LibreOffice Base	Provides dialogs to set and edit connections and registered databases.	Base
Charts	Defines the default colors used for newly created charts.	All
Internet	Allows configuring a proxy and the e-mail software to use. You can also enable viewing LibreOffice documents in Firefox.	All

🛈 Important: Settings Apply Globally

All settings listed in the table apply *globally* for the specified applications. That means, they are used as defaults for every new document you create.

8.8 Using Templates

A template is a document containing only the styles—and content— that you want to appear in every document of that type. When a document is created or opened with the template, the styles are automatically applied to that document. Templates greatly enhance the use of LibreOffice by simplifying formatting tasks for a variety of different types of documents.

For example, in a word processor, you can write letters, memos, and reports, all of which look different and require different styles. Or, for example, for spreadsheets, you could use different cell styles or headings for certain types of spreadsheets. If you use templates for each of your document types, the styles you need for each document are always readily available.

LibreOffice comes with a set of predefined templates, and you can find additional templates on the Internet. For details, see *Section 8.10, "For More Information"*. If you want to create your own templates, this requires some up-front planning. You need to determine how you want the document to look so you can create the styles you need in that template.

A detailed explanation of templates is beyond the scope of this section. *Procedure 8.6, "Creating LibreOffice Templates"* only shows how to generate a template from an existing document.

PROCEDURE 8.6: CREATING LIBREOFFICE TEMPLATES

For text documents, spreadsheets, presentations, and drawings, you can easily create a template from an existing document as follows:

1. Start LibreOffice and open or create a document that contains the styles and content that you want to re-use for other documents of that type.

2. Click *File › Templates › Save as Template*.

3. Choose a directory to save the image in by double-clicking one of the directory names. If you are in a subdirectory and want to go up again, use the path bar displayed above the directories.

4. From the toolbar, choose *Save*.

5. Specify a name for the template.

6. Click *OK*.

Note: Converting Microsoft Word Templates

You can convert Microsoft Word templates like you would convert any other Word document. For more information, see *Section 8.3.1, "Converting Documents to the LibreOffice Format".*

8.9 Setting Metadata and Properties

When exchanging documents with other people, it is sometimes useful to store metadata like the owner of the file, who it was received from, and a URL. LibreOffice lets you attach such metadata to the file. This helps you track metadata which you do not want to or cannot save in the content of the file. This feature is also the basis for later sorting, searching and retrieving your documents based on metadata.

As an example, we assume you want to set these properties to your file:

- A title, subject, and some keywords

- The owner of the file

- Who sent you the file

To attach such metadata to your document, proceed as follows:

PROCEDURE 8.7: SETTING PROPERTIES

1. Click *File* › *Properties*. A dialog opens. It has, among others, the following tabs:

   Description
   > Insert your title, subject, keywords and comments as you like.

   Custom Properties
   > Custom properties specify the editor, owner, publisher, received from, and other useful metadata.

2. Change to the *Description* tab and insert title, subject, and your keywords.

3. Switch to the *Custom Properties* tab.

4. In the *Name* row, click the drop-down box of an unused entry (for example, `Info 1`). A list of properties appears, from it, choose *Owner*.

5. Insert the name of the owner in the *Value* row.

6. Repeat the previous step with the *Received from* property and a suitable value.

7. If you want to add more than four properties, use *Add* to add another row.

8. Leave the dialog with *OK*.

9. Save your file.

8.10 For More Information

LibreOffice contains extensive online help. In addition, a large community of users and developers support it. The following lists shows some places where you can go for additional information.

LibreOffice Online Help Menu

Extensive help on performing any task in LibreOffice.

http://www.libreoffice.org

Home page of LibreOffice

http://ask.libreoffice.org

Official question and answer page for LibreOffice.

http://www.taming-libreoffice.com/

Taming LibreOffice: books, news, tips and tricks.

http://www.pitonyak.org/oo.php

Extensive information about creating and using macros.

http://www.worldlabel.com/Pages/openoffice-template.htm

Various templates for creating labels with LibreOffice.

9 LibreOffice Writer

LibreOffice Writer is a full-featured word processor with page and text formatting capabilities. Its interface is similar to interfaces of other major word processors, and it includes some features that are usually found only in desktop publishing applications.

This chapter highlights a few key features of Writer. For more information about these features and for complete instructions for using Writer, look at the LibreOffice help or at the sources listed in *Section 8.10, "For More Information"*.

Much of the information in this chapter can also be applied to other LibreOffice modules. For example, other modules use styles similarly to how they are used in Writer.

9.1 Creating a New Document

There are three ways to create a new Writer document.

- **From Scratch.** To create a document from scratch, click *File* › *New* › *Text Document* and a new empty Writer document is created.

- **Wizard.** To use a standard format and predefined elements for your own documents, use a wizard. Click *File* › *Wizards* › *Letter* and follow the steps.

- **Templates.** To use a template, click *File* › *New* › *Templates* and choose one of the directories (for example, `Business Correspondence`) and a new document based on the style of your selected template is created.

For example, to create a business letter, click *File* › *Wizards* › *Letter*. Using the wizard's dialogs, you can easily create a basic document using a standard format. A sample wizard dialog is shown in *Figure 9.1*.

Steps

1. Page design
2. Letterhead layout
3. Printed items
4. Recipient and sender
5. Footer
6. Name and location

Please choose the type of letter and page design

○ Business letter

    Page design   Elegant

        ☐ Use letterhead paper with pre-printed elements

○ Formal personal letter

    Page design   Elegant

○ Personal letter

    Page design   Bottle

💡 This wizard helps you to create a letter template. You can then use the template as the basis for writing letters as often as desired.

Help   < Back   Next >   Finish   Cancel

FIGURE 9.1: A LIBREOFFICE WIZARD

Enter text in the document window as desired. Use the *Formatting* toolbar or the *Format* menu to adjust the appearance of the document. Use the *File* menu or the relevant buttons in the toolbar to print and save your document. With the options under *Insert*, add extra items to your document, such as a table, picture, or chart.

9.2   Sharing Documents with Other Word Processors

You can use Writer to edit documents created in a variety of other word processors. For example, you can import a Microsoft* Word* document, edit it, and save it again as a Microsoft Word document. If you use LibreOffice in an environment where you need to share documents with Microsoft Word users, you should have little or no trouble exchanging document files.

Most Microsoft Word documents can be opened in LibreOffice without issue. Formatting, fonts, and all other aspects of the document remain intact. However, very complex documents can require editing after opening. Complex documents are documents containing, for example, complicated tables, Microsoft Office macros, or unusual fonts and formatting.

LibreOffice can save many popular word processing formats. Documents created in LibreOffice and saved as Microsoft Word files can be opened in Microsoft Word.

9.3 Formatting with Styles

The traditional way of formatting office documents is direct formatting. That means, you use a button, such as *Bold*, which sets a certain property (in this case, a bold typeface). With styles, you can bundle a set of properties (for example, font size and font weight) and give them a speaking name, such as *Headline, first level*. Using styles, rather than direct formatting has the following advantages:

- Gives your pages, paragraphs, texts, and lists a consistent look.

- Makes it easy to consistently change formatting later.

- Reuse and load styles from another document.

- Change one style and its properties are passed on to its descendants.

For example, imagine that you emphasize text by selecting it and clicking the *Bold* button. Later, decide you want the emphasized text to be italicized. Now, you would need to find all bolded text and manually change it to italics. If you use a character style from the beginning, however, you only need to change the style from bold to italics once. All text that has been formatted with that style then changes from bold to italics.

LibreOffice can use styles for applying consistent formatting to various elements in a document. The following types of styles are available in Writer:

TABLE 9.1: TYPES OF STYLES

Type of Style	What it Does
Paragraph	Applies standardized formatting to the various types of paragraphs in your document. For example, apply a paragraph style to a first-level heading to set the font and font size, spacing above and below the heading, location of the heading, and other formatting specifications.
Character	Applies standardized formatting for types of text. For example, if you want emphasized text to appear in italics, you can create an emphasis style that italicizes selected text when you apply the style to it.

Type of Style	What it Does
Frame	Applies standardized formatting to frames. For example, if your document uses marginal notes, you can create frames with specified borders, location, and other formatting so that all of your marginal notes have a consistent appearance.
Page	Applies standardized formatting to a specified type of page. For example, if every page of your document contains a header and footer except for the first page, you can use a first page style that disables headers and footers. You can also use different page styles for left and right pages so that you have bigger margins on the insides of pages and your page numbers appear on an outside corner.
List	Applies standardized formatting to specified list types. For example, you can define a checklist with square check boxes and a bullet list with round bullets, then easily apply the correct style when creating your lists.

Text that is formatted with a menu option or toolbar button overrides any styles you have applied. For example, format a piece of text both with a character style and using the *Bold* button. Now, the text will be bold, no matter what is set in the style.

To remove all direct formatting, first select the appropriate text, then right-click it and choose *Clear Direct Formatting*.

Likewise, if you manually format paragraphs using *Format › Paragraph*, you can easily end up with inconsistent paragraph formatting. This is especially true if you copy and paste paragraphs from other documents with different formatting. However, if you apply paragraph styles, formatting remains consistent. If you change a style, the change is automatically applied to all paragraphs formatted with that style.

9.3.1 The Styles and Formatting Window

The *Styles and Formatting* window is a versatile formatting tool for applying styles to text, paragraphs, pages, frames, and lists. To open this window, click *Format › Styles and Formatting* or press `F11`.

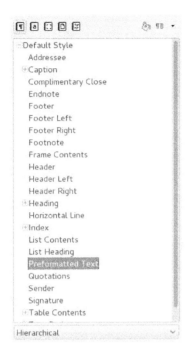

FIGURE 9.2: STYLES AND FORMATTING WINDOW

 Tip: Docking And Undocking the Style and Formatting Window

By default, the *Styles and Formatting* window is a floating window. It opens in its own window that you can place anywhere on the screen.

To make it appear always in the same part of the Writer interface, you can *dock* the *Styles and Formatting* window. To do so, drag its titlebar to the left or right side of the main Writer window until a gray frame appears, then release the mouse button to position it there. To undock the window and make it appear as a floating window again, drag its icon bar to a different place.

The docking/undocking mechanism applies to some other windows in LibreOffice as well, including the Navigator.

LibreOffice comes with several predefined styles. You can use these styles as they are, modify them, or create new styles. Use the icons at the top of the window to display formatting styles for the most common elements like paragraphs, frames, pages or lists. Go on with the instructions below, to learn more about styles.

9.3.2 Applying a Style

To apply a style, select the element you want to apply the style to, and double-click the style in the *Styles and Formatting* window. For example, to apply a style to a paragraph, place the cursor anywhere in that paragraph and double-click the desired paragraph style.

9.3.3 Changing a Style

By changing styles you can change formatting throughout a document, rather than applying the change separately everywhere you want to apply the new formatting.

To change an existing style, proceed as follows:

1. In the *Styles and Formatting* window, right-click the style you want to change.

2. Click *Modify*.

3. Change the settings for the selected style.
   For information about the available settings, refer to the LibreOffice online help.

4. Click *OK*.

9.3.4 Creating a Style

LibreOffice comes with a collection of styles to suit many users' needs. However, most users eventually need a style that does not yet exist and therefore, want to create their own style:

PROCEDURE 9.1: GENERAL APPROACH FOR CREATING A NEW STYLE

1. Open the *Styles and Formatting* window with *Format › Styles and Formatting*, or press `F11`.

2. Make sure you are in the list of styles for the type of style you want to create.
   For example, if you are creating a character style, make sure you are in the character style list by clicking the corresponding icon in the *Styles and Formatting* window.

3. Right-click anywhere in the list of styles in the *Styles and Formatting* window.

4. Click *New* and the style dialog opens. The *Organizer* tab is preselected.

5. First configure the three most important entries:

Name

> The name of your style. Choose any name you like.

Next Style

> The style that follows your style. The style here is used, when starting a new paragraph by pressing `Enter`. This is useful, for example, for headlines, after which you usually want to start a normal paragraph of text.

Inherit From

> A style that your style depends on. If the selected style is changed, your style changes as well. For example, if you want to make consistent headers create a "parent" header style and subsequent headers depending on it. This can be useful when you only want to change the properties that need to be different.

> For details about the style options available in any tab, click that tab and then click *Help*.

6. Confirm with *OK* to close the window.

9.3.4.1   Example: Defining a Note Style

Let us assume, you need a note with a different background and borders. To create such styles, proceed as follows:

PROCEDURE 9.2: CREATING A NOTE STYLE

1. Press `F11`. The *Styles and Formatting* window opens.

2. Make sure you are in the *Paragraph Style* list by checking the pilcrow icon (¶) is selected.

3. Right-click anywhere in the list of styles in the *Styles and Formatting* window and select *New*.

4. Enter the following parameters in the *Organizer* tab:

Name	Note
Next Style	Note
Inherit from	- None -

Category	Custom Styles

5. Change the indentation in the *Indents & Spacing* tab, labeled with *Before Text*. If you want more space above and below individual paragraphs, change the values in the *Above paragraph* and *Below paragraph* accordingly.

6. Switch to the *Background* tab and choose a color for the background.

7. Switch to the *Borders* tab and determine your line arrangements, line style, color and other parameters.

8. Confirm with *OK* to close the window.

9. Select your text in your document and double-click the *Note* style. Your style parameters are applied to the text.

9.3.4.2 Example: Defining an Even-Odd Page Style

If you want to create double-sided printouts of your documents, it is a good idea to create even and odd pages. To create page styles for this, proceed as follows:

PROCEDURE 9.3: CREATE AN EVEN (LEFT) PAGE STYLE

1. Press F11. The *Styles and Formatting* window opens.

2. Make sure you are in the *Page Style* list by checking that the paper sheet icon is selected.

3. Right-click anywhere in the list of styles in the *Styles and Formatting* window and select *New*.

4. Enter the following parameters in the *Organizer* tab:

Name	Left Content Page
Next Style	Leave empty, will be changed later
Inherit from	not applicable
Category	not applicable

5. Change additional parameters as you like in the other tabs. You can also adapt the page format and margins (*Page* tab) or any headers and footers.

6. Confirm with *OK* to close the window.

PROCEDURE 9.4: CREATE AN ODD (RIGHT) PAGE STYLE

1. Follow the instruction in *Procedure 9.3, "Create an Even (Left) Page Style"* but use the string `Right Content Page` in the *Organizer* tab.

2. Select the entry *Left Content Page* from the *Next Style* pop-up menu.

3. Choose the same parameters as you did in the left page style. If you used different sizes for the left and right margin of your even page, you should mirror these values in your odd pages.

4. Confirm with *OK* to close the window.

Then connect the left page style with the right page style:

PROCEDURE 9.5: CONNECT THE RIGHT PAGE STYLE WITH THE LEFT PAGE STYLE

1. Right-click the *Left Content Page* entry and choose *Modify*.

2. Choose *Right Content Page* from the *Next Style* pop-up menu.

3. Confirm with *OK* to close the window.

To attach your style, make sure your page is a left (even) page and double-click *Left Content Page*. Whenever your text exceeds the length of a page, the following page automatically receives the alternative page style.

9.4   Working with Large Documents

You can use Writer to work on large documents. Large documents can be either a single file or a collection of files assembled into a single document.

9.4.1   Navigating in Large Documents

The Navigator tool displays information about the contents of a document. It also lets you quickly jump to different elements. For example, you can use the Navigator to get a quick overview of all images included in a document.

To open the Navigator, click *View* › *Navigator* or press F5 . The elements listed in the Navigator vary according to the document loaded in Writer.

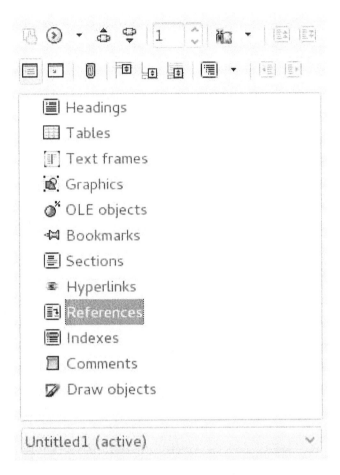

FIGURE 9.3: NAVIGATOR TOOL IN WRITER

Double-click an item in the Navigator to jump to that item in the document.

9.4.2 Using Master Documents

If you are working with a very large document, such as a book, you might find it easier to manage the book with a master document, rather than keeping the book in a single file. A master document enables you to quickly apply formatting changes to a large document or to jump to each subdocument for editing.

A master document is a Writer document that serves as a container for multiple Writer files. You can maintain chapters or other subdocuments as individual files collected in the master document. Master documents are also useful if multiple users are working on a single document.

You can separate each user's section of the document into subdocuments collected in a master document, allowing multiple writers to work on their subdocuments at the same time without fear of overwriting others' work.

PROCEDURE 9.6: CREATING A MASTER DOCUMENT

1. Click *New* › *Master Document*.

   or

   Open an existing document and click *File* › *Send* › *Create Master Document*.

2. The *Navigator* window will open. In it, select *Insert* (), then choose *File*.

3. Select a file to add an existing file to the master document.

To enter some text directly into the master document, select *Insert* › *Text*.

The LibreOffice help files contain more complete information about working with master documents. Look for the topic named *Using Master Documents and Subdocuments*.

Tip: Styles and Templates in Master Documents

The styles from all of your subdocuments are imported into the master document. To ensure that formatting is consistent throughout your master document, you should use the same template for each subdocument. Doing so is not mandatory. However, if subdocuments are formatted differently, you might need to do some reformatting to successfully bring subdocuments into the master document without creating inconsistencies. For example, if two documents imported into your master document include different styles with the same name, the master document will use the formatting specified for that style in the first document you import.

9.5 Using Writer as an HTML Editor

In addition to being a full-featured word processor, Writer also functions as an HTML editor. You can style HTML pages like any other document, but there are specific *HTML Styles* that help with creating good HTML. You can view the document as it will appear online, or you can directly edit the HTML code.

PROCEDURE 9.7: CREATING AN HTML PAGE

1. Click *File > New > HTML Document*.

2. Press F11 to open the *Styles and Formatting* window.

3. At the bottom of the *Styles and Formatting* window, click the drop-down box to open it.

4. Select *HTML Styles*.

5. Create your HTML page, using the styles to tag your text.

6. Click *File > Save As*.

7. Select the location where you want to save your file and name the file. Make sure that in the bottom drop-down box, *HTML Document* is selected.

8. Click *OK*.

If you prefer to edit HTML code directly, or if you want to see the HTML code created when you edit the HTML file as a Writer document, click *View > HTML Source*. In HTML Source mode, the *Formatting and Styles* list is not available.

The first time you switch to HTML Source mode, you are prompted to save the file as HTML, if you have not already done so.

To switch back from HTML Source mode to Web Layout, click *View > HTML source* again.

10 LibreOffice Calc

Calc is the LibreOffice spreadsheet and data plotting module. Spreadsheets consist of several sheets, containing cells which can be filled with elements like text, numbers, or formulas. A formula can manipulate data from other cells to generate a value for the cell in which it is inserted. Calc also allows you to define ranges, filter and sort the data or creates charts from the data to present it graphically. By using pivot tables, you can combine, analyze or compare larger amounts of data.

As with the entire LibreOffice suite, Calc can be used across a variety of platforms. It provides several exchange formats (including export to PDF documents), and can also read and save files in Microsoft Excel format. Its interoperability is constantly ameliorated.

This chapter can only introduce some very basic Calc functionality. For more information and for complete instructions, look at the LibreOffice help or at the sources listed in *Section 8.10, "For More Information"*.

 Note: VBA Macros

Calc can process many VBA macros in Excel documents. However, support for VBA macros is not yet complete. When opening an Excel spreadsheet that makes heavy use of macros, you might discover that some do not work.

10.1 Creating a New Document

There are two ways to create a new Calc document:

- **From Scratch.** To create a document from scratch, click *File* › *New* › *Spreadsheet* and a new empty Calc document is created.

- **Templates.** To use a template, click *File* › *New* › *Templates* and open *Finances*. You can see a list of Spreadsheet templates. Select the one that fits your needs and your new document is created based on the style of your selected template.

Access the individual sheets by clicking the respective tabs at the bottom of the window.

Enter data in the cells as desired. To adjust the appearance, either use the *Formatting* toolbar or the *Format* menu—or define styles as described in *Section 10.2, "Using Formatting and Styles in Calc"*. Use the *File* menu or the relevant buttons in the toolbar to print and save your document.

10.2 Using Formatting and Styles in Calc

Calc comes with a few built-in cell and page styles to improve the appearance of your spreadsheets and reports. Although these built-in styles are adequate for many uses, you will probably find it useful to create styles for your own frequently used formatting preferences.

PROCEDURE 10.1: CREATING A STYLE

1. Click *Format > Styles and Formatting*.

2. In the *Styles and Formatting* window, click either the *Cell Styles* or the *Page Styles* icon from the top of the window.

3. Right-click anywhere in the list of styles in the *Styles and Formatting* window. Then click *New*.

4. Specify a name for your style and use the various tabs to set the desired formatting options.

5. Click *OK*.

PROCEDURE 10.2: MODIFYING A STYLE

1. Click *Format > Styles and Formatting*.

2. In the *Formatting and Styles* window, click either the *Cell Styles* or the *Page Styles* icon.

3. Right-click the name of the style you want to change, then click *Modify*.

4. Change the desired formatting options.

5. Click OK.

To apply a style to specific cells, select the cells you want to format. Then double-click the style you want to apply in the *Styles and Formatting* window.

10.3 Working With Sheets

Sheets are a good method to organize your calculations. For example, if you have a business, accounting might be much clearer if you create a sheet for each month.

To insert a new sheet in your spreadsheet, do the following:

PROCEDURE 10.3: INSERTING NEW SHEETS

1. Select *Insert > Sheet* from the main menu. A dialog opens.

2. Decide whether the new sheet should be positioned before or after the selected sheet.

3. If you want to create a new sheet, make sure the *New Sheet* radio button is activated. Enter the number of sheets and the sheet name. Skip the next step.

4. If you want to import a sheet from another file, do the following otherwise skip this step:

   a. Select *From file* and click *Browse*.

   b. Select the file name and confirm with *OK*. All the sheet names are now displayed in the list.

   c. Select the sheet names you want to import by holding the `Shift` key.

   d. Confirm with *OK* to import the sheet names you selected.

To rename a sheet, right-click a sheet in the sheet tab and select *Rename Sheet*. To rename, you can also double-click the sheet tab.

To delete the current sheet, select *Edit › Sheet › Delete* and confirm with *Delete Sheets*. It is possible to delete more than one sheet by holding the `Shift` key and selecting the sheets you want to delete in the sheet tab. Right-click and choose *Delete Sheet* and the same dialog appears. Confirm with *Delete Sheets*.

10.4   Conditional Formatting

Conditional formatting is a useful feature to highlight certain values in your spreadsheet. For example, define a condition and if the condition is true, a style is applied to each cell that fulfills this condition.

 Note: Enable AutoCalculate

> Before you apply conditional formatting, choose *Tools › Cell Contents › AutoCalculate*. You should see a check mark in front of *AutoCalculate*.

PROCEDURE 10.4: USING CONDITIONAL FORMATTING

1. Define a style first. This style is applied to each cell when your condition is true. Use *Format › Styles and Formatting* or press `F11`. For more information, see *Procedure 10.1, "Creating a Style"*. Confirm with *OK*.

2. Select the cell range where you want to apply your condition.

3. Select *Format* › *Conditional Formatting* › *Condition* from the main menu. A dialog opens.

4. You now see a template for a new condition. Conditions can operate in multiple modes:

    Cell value is

    > The condition tests if a cell matches a certain value. Beside the first pull-down menu, you can select an operator such as *equal to, less than,* or *greater than*.

    Formula is

    > The condition tests if a certain formula returns true.

    Date is

    > The condition tests if a certain date value is reached.

    All Cells

    > This mode allows creating data visualizations that, similarly to *Cell value is*, depend on the value of a cell. However, the difference here is that you can use one condition to apply an entire range of styles.

5. For this example, keep the default: *Cell value is*.

6. Select an operator and the value of the cell you want to test for.

7. Choose the style you want to apply when this condition is true or click *New Style* to define a new appearance.

8. If you need additional conditions, click *Add*. Then repeat the previous steps.

9. Confirm with *OK*. Now the style of your cells has changed.

10.5 Grouping and Ungrouping Cells

Grouping a cell range helps to fold your spreadsheet into parts. This makes your spreadsheets more readable, as you can hide all the parts you are not currently interested in. It is possible to group rows or columns and nest groups in other groups.

To group a range, proceed as follows:

PROCEDURE 10.5: GROUPING A SELECTED CELL RANGE

1. Select a cell range in your spreadsheet.

2. Select *Data* › *Group and Outline* › *Group*. A dialog appears.

3. Decide if you want to group your selected range as row or as column. Confirm with *OK*.

After grouping selected cells, a line indicating the grouped cell range appears in the upper-left margin. Fold or unfold the cell range with the + and - icons. The numbers at the top left of the margins display the depth of your groups and can be clicked too.

To ungroup a cell range, click into a cell which belongs to a group and select *Data* › *Group and Outline* › *Ungroup*. The line in the margin disappears. The innermost group is always deleted first.

10.6   Freezing Rows or Columns as Headers

If you have a spreadsheet with lots of data, scrolling makes your header usually disappear. LibreOffice can lock rows or columns or both, so they remain fixed as you scroll around.

To freeze a single row or a single column, proceed as follows:

PROCEDURE 10.6: FREEZING A SINGLE ROW OR COLUMN

1. To create a frozen area before a row, click the header of the row (1, 2, 3, ...).
   To create a frozen area above a column, click the header of the column (A, B, C, ...).

2. Select *Window* › *Freeze*. A dark line appears, indicating which area is frozen.

It is also possible to freeze both rows and columns:

PROCEDURE 10.7: FREEZING ROW AND COLUMN

1. Click into the cell to the right of the column and below the row you want frozen. For example, if your header occupies the space from A1 to B3, click cell C4.

2. Select *Window* › *Freeze*. A dark line appears, indicating which area is frozen.

To unfreeze, select *Window* › *Freeze*. The check mark in the menu then disappears.

11 LibreOffice Impress, Base, Draw, and Math

Besides LibreOffice Writer and LibreOffice Calc, LibreOffice also includes the modules Impress, Base, Draw, and Math. With these you can create presentations, design databases, draw up graphics and diagrams, and create mathematical formulas.

11.1 Using Presentations with Impress

Use LibreOffice Impress to create presentations for screen display or printing. If you have used other presentation software, Impress makes it easy to switch. It works very similarly to other presentation software.

Impress can open and save Microsoft* PowerPoint* presentations. This means you can exchange presentations with PowerPoint* users, as long as you save your presentations in PowerPoint* format.

11.1.1 Creating a Presentation

There are multiple ways to create a new Impress document:

- **From Scratch.** To create a document from scratch, click *File* › *New* › *Presentation* and a new empty Impress document is created.

- **Wizard.** To use a standard format and predefined elements for your documents use a wizard. Click *File* › *Wizards* › *Presentation* and follow the steps.

- **Templates.** To use a template, click *File* › *New* › *Templates* and choose a template from *Presentation Backgrounds*. A new document based on the style of your selected template is created.

The following procedure describes how to create a presentation by using the wizard. Proceed as follows:

1. Start LibreOffice.

2. Select *File* › *Wizards* › *Presentation*

3. Choose *From template* and select *Presentation Backgrounds* from the pop-up menu to set your preferred background and click *Next*.

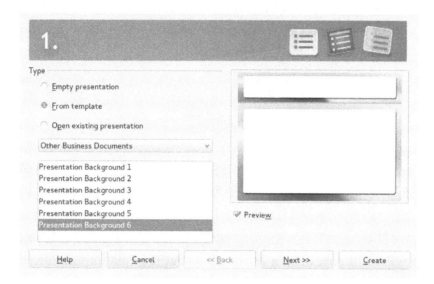

4. Select an output medium. The output medium is the form the final presentation will take, such as: *Overhead sheet, Paper*, a slideshow on a 4:3 *Screen* or a 16:9 *Widescreen*, among other choices.

Select *Preview* for a thumbnail showing your choices. If all options are set according to your wishes, click *Next*.

5. If you want to use effects for slide transitions, select the *Effect* you want to use and specify the *Speed*. The effect will be previewed immediately.

6. Either use the default presentation type or choose *Automatic* to specify the amount of time each page displays and the length of the pause between presentations.

7. If all options are set according to your wishes, click *Create*.

The presentation opens, ready for editing.

11.1.2   Using Master Pages

Master pages give your presentation a consistent look by defining what fonts and other design elements are used. Impress uses two types of master pages:

Slide Master

> Contains elements that appear on all slides. For example, you might want your company logo to appear in the same place on every slide. The slide master also determines the text formatting style for the heading and outline of every slide that uses that master page, as well as any information you want to appear in a header or footer.

Notes Master

> Determines the formatting and appearance of the notes in your presentation.

11.1.2.1   Creating a Slide Master

Impress comes with a collection of preformatted master pages. Eventually, many users will want to customize their presentations by creating their own slide masters.

1. Start Impress.

2. To create a new empty presentation, select *File › New › Presentation*.

3. Click *View › Master › Slide Master*.
   This opens the current slide master in *Master View*. The *Master View* toolbar appears.

4. Right-click the left-hand panel, then click *New Master*.

5. Edit the slide master until it has the desired look.
   A special feature of Master View is that you can edit outline styles by directly formatting the sample text on the slide.

6. To finish editing slide masters, in the *Master View* toolbar, click *Close Master View*. Alternatively, choose *View › Normal*.

> **Tip: Collect Slide Masters in a Template**
>
> When you have created all of the slide masters you want to use in your presentations, you can save them in an Impress template. Then, any time you want to create presentations that use those slide masters, open a new presentation with your template.

11.1.2.2 Applying a Slide Master

Slide masters can be applied to selected slides or to all slides in the presentation.

1. Open your presentation.

2. (Optional) If you want to apply the slide master to multiple slides, but not to all slides. Select the slides that you want to use that slide master applied to.

   To select multiple slides, press Ctrl in the *Slides Pane* while clicking the slides you want to use.

3. In the Tasks Pane, open the *Master Pages* and click the master page you want to apply. The slide master is applied to the corresponding page(s).

   If you do not see the *Task Pane,* click *View › Task Pane.*

11.2 Using Databases with Base

LibreOffice includes the database module Base. Use Base to design a database to store many different kinds of information. From a simple address book or recipe file to a sophisticated document management system.

Tables, forms, queries, and reports can be created manually or by using convenient wizards. For example, the Table Wizard contains several common fields for business and personal use. Databases created in Base can be used as data sources, such as when creating form letters.

It is beyond the scope of this document to detail database design with Base. More information can be found at the sources listed in *Section 8.10, "For More Information".*

11.2.1 Creating a Database Using Predefined Options

Base comes with several predefined database fields to help you create a database. A wizard guides you through the steps to create a new database. The steps in this section are specific to creating an address book using predefined fields, but it should be easy to follow them to use the predefined fields for any of the built-in database options.

The process for creating a database can be broken into several subprocesses:

1. *Creating the Database*

2. *Setting Up the Database Table*

3. *Creating a Form*

4. *Modifying the Form*

11.2.1.1   Creating the Database

1. Start LibreOffice Base.

2. Select *Create a new database*.

3. You can choose between creating an HSQLDB or Firebird database.

   HSQLDB Embedded *(default)*

   > This database format is also available in older versions of OpenOffice.org and Libre-Office. It depends on Java being installed on the computer.

   Firebird Embedded

   > This database format can only be used in newer versions of LibreOffice. It does not depend on Java. When you do large database operations, Firebird can perform better.

4. Proceed with *Next*.

5. Click *Yes, register the database for me* to make your database information available to other LibreOffice modules and select the check boxes to *Open the database for editing* and *Create tables using the table wizard*. Then click *Finish*.

6. Browse to the directory where you want to save the database, specify a name for the database, then click *OK*.

11.2.1.2   Setting Up the Database Table

After you have created the database, if you have selected the *Create tables using the table wizard* check box, the table wizard opens. If you have not, click the *Use Wizard to Create Table* link in the *Tasks* area. Next, define the fields you want to use in your database table.

1. In the *Table Wizard*, click *Personal*.
   The *Sample tables* list changes to show the predefined tables for personal use. If you had clicked *Business*, the list would contain predefined business tables.

2. In the *Sample tables* list, click *Addresses*.

The available fields for the predefined address book appear in the *Available fields* menu.

3. In the *Available fields* menu, click the fields you want to use in your address book.

   You can select one item at a time, or you can shift-click multiple items to select them.

4. Click the single arrow icon to move the selected items to the *Selected fields* menu.

   To move all available fields to the *Selected fields* menu, click the double right-arrow.

5. Use the ⬆ and ⬇ keys to adjust the order of the selected fields, then click *Next*.

   The fields appear in the table and forms in the order in which they are listed.

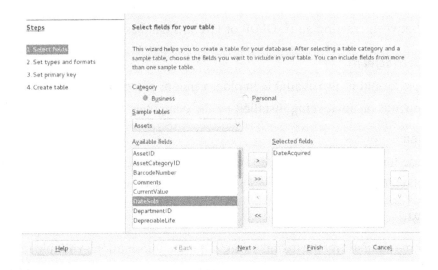

6. Make sure each of the fields is defined correctly.

   You can change the field name, type, maximum characters and whether it is a required field. For this example, leave the settings as they are, then click *Next*.

7. Click *Create a primary key*, click *Automatically add a primary key*, click *Auto value*, then click *Next*.

11.2.1.3   Creating a Form

Next, create the form to use when entering data into your address book.

1. In the *Form Wizard*, click the double right-arrow icon to move all available fields to the *Fields in the form* list, then click *Next*.

2. Select *Add Subform* if you want to add a subform, then click *Next*.

   For this example, accept the default selections.

3. Select how you want to arrange your form, then click *Next.*

4. Select *The form is to display all data* and leave all of the check boxes empty, then click *Next.*

5. Apply a style and field border, then click *Next.*
For this example, accept the default selections.

6. Name the form, select the *Modify the form* option, then click *Finish.*

11.2.1.4 Modifying the Form

After the form has been defined, you can modify the appearance of the form to suit your preferences.

1. Close the form that opened when you finished the previous step.

2. In the main window for your database, right-click the form you want to modify (there should be only one option), then click *Edit.*

3. Arrange the fields on the form by dragging them to their new locations.
For example, move the First Name field so it appears to the right of the Last Name field, and then adjust the locations of the other fields to suit your preference.

4. When you have finished modifying the form, save it and close it.

11.2.1.5 Further Steps

After you have created your database tables and forms, you are ready to enter your data. You can also design queries and reports to help sort and display the data.

Refer to LibreOffice online help and other sources listed in *Section 8.10, "For More Information"* for additional information about Base.

11.3 Creating Graphics with Draw

Use LibreOffice Draw to create graphics and diagrams. You can export your drawings to the most common vector graphics formats and import them into any application that lets you import graphics, including other LibreOffice modules. You can also create Adobe* Flash* (SWF) versions of your drawings.

1. Start LibreOffice Draw.

2. Use the toolbar at the bottom of the window to create a graphic.

3. Save the graphic.

To embed an existing Draw graphic into a LibreOffice document, select *Insert › Object › OLE Object*. Select *Create from file* and click *Search* to navigate to the Draw file to insert. If you insert a file as OLE object, you can easily edit the object later by double-clicking it.

PROCEDURE 11.2: OPENING DRAW FROM OTHER LIBREOFFICE MODULES

One particularly useful feature of Draw is the ability to open it from other LibreOffice modules, so you can create a drawing that is automatically imported into your document.

1. From a LibreOffice module (for example, from Writer), click *Insert › Object › OLE Object › LibreOffice 3.x Drawing › OK*.
   The user interface of Writer will now be replaced by that of Draw.

2. Create your drawing.

3. Click in your document, outside the Draw frame.
   The drawing is automatically inserted into your document.

11.4   Creating Mathematical Formulas with Math

It is usually difficult to include complex mathematical formulas in your documents. To make this task easier, the LibreOffice Math equation editor lets you create formulas using operators, functions, and formatting assistants. You can then save those formulas as an object that can be imported into other documents. Math functions can be inserted into other LibreOffice documents like any other graphic object.

 Note: Math is For Creating Mathematical Formulas

Math is not a calculator. The functions it creates are graphical objects. Even if they are imported into Calc, these functions cannot be evaluated.

To create a formula proceed as follows:

1. Start LibreOffice Math.

2. Click *File* › *New* › *Formula*. The formula window opens.

3. Enter your formula in the lower part of the window. For example, the binomial theorem in LibreOffice Math syntax is:

   ```
   (a + b)^2 = a^2 + 2 a b + b^2
   ```

   The result is displayed in the upper part of the window.

4. Use the *Formula Elements* window or right-click the lower part of the window to insert other terms. If you need symbols, use *Tools* › *Catalog* to, for example, insert Greek or other special characters.

5. Save your document.

The result is shown in *Figure 11.1, "Mathematical Formula in LibreOffice Math"*:

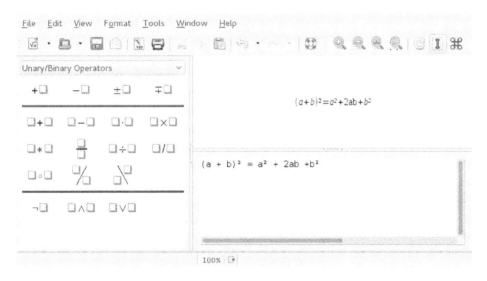

FIGURE 11.1: MATHEMATICAL FORMULA IN LIBREOFFICE MATH

It is possible to include your formula in Writer, for example. To do so, proceed as follows:

1. Create a new Writer document or open an already existing one.

2. Select *Insert* › *Object* › *OLE Object* in the main menu. The *Insert OLE Object* window appears.

3. Select *Create from file*.

Creating Mathematical Formulas with Math   SLED 12 SP1

4. Click *Search* to locate your formula. If needed, you can activate *Link to file*.

5. Confirm with *OK* and your formula is inserted at the current cursor position.

IV Information Management

12 Evolution: E-Mailing and Calendaring

Evolution makes storing, organizing, and retrieving your personal information easy, so you can work and communicate more effectively with others. It is a professional groupware program and an important part of the Internet-connected desktop.

Evolution can help you work in a group by handling e-mail, contact information, and one or more calendars. It can do that on one or several computers, connected directly or over a network, for one person or for large groups.

Evolution helps you accomplish common daily tasks quickly. For example, you can easily reuse appointment or contact information sent to you by e-mail, or send e-mail to a contact or appointment. If you receive lots of e-mail, you can use advanced features like search folders, which let you save searches as though they were ordinary e-mail folders.

This chapter introduces you to Evolution and helps you get started. For more details, refer to the Evolution application help.

12.1 Starting Evolution

To start Evolution, click *Applications* › *Internet* › *Evolution*.

12.2 Setup Assistant

The first time you start Evolution, it opens an assistant to help you set up e-mail accounts and import data from other applications.

The *Evolution Account Assistant* helps you provide all the required information.

12.2.1 Restoring from a Backup File

When the assistant starts, the *Welcome* page is displayed. Click *Continue* to proceed to the *Restore from Backup* page. If you previously backed up your Evolution configuration and want to restore it, check *Restore Evolution from the Backup File*. Then, select the backup file in the file chooser dialog.

Otherwise, click *Continue* and proceed to *Identity*.

12.2.2 Defining Your Identity

The *Identity* page is the next step in the assistant.

1. Type your full name in the *Full Name* field.

2. Type your e-mail address in the *E-mail Address* field.

3. (Optional) Type a reply to address in the *Reply-To* field.
   Only use this field if you want replies to e-mails from you to be sent to a different e-mail address.

4. (Optional) Type your organization name in the *Organization* field.
   This is the company where you work, or the organization you represent when you send e-mails.

5. Click *Continue*.

12.2.3 Receiving Mail

The *Receiving E-mail* page lets you determine the server that you want to use to receive e-mail.

You need to specify the type of server you want to receive mail from. If you are not sure about the type of server, contact your system administrator or e-mail provider.

Select a server type in the *Server Type* list. The following is a list of available server types:

Exchange Web Services: Allows you to connect to newer Microsoft Exchange servers to synchronize e-mail, calendar, and contact information. This is only available if you have installed the connector for Microsoft* Exchange* which is packaged in `evolution-ews`.

IMAP+: Keeps the e-mail on your server, so you can access your e-mail from multiple systems.

POP: Downloads your e-mail to your hard disk for permanent storage, freeing up space on the e-mail server.

USENET News: Connects to a news server and downloads a list of available news digests.

Local Delivery: If you want to move e-mail from the spool and store it in your home directory, you need to provide the path to the mail spool you want to use. If you want to leave mail in your system's spool files, select *Standard Unix Mbox Spool File* instead.

MH Format Mail Directories: To download your e-mail using **mh** or an **mh** -style program, you need to provide the path to the mail directory you want to use.

Maildir Format Mail Directories: If you download your e-mail using Qmail or another Maildir-style program, select this option. You need to provide the path to the mail directory you want to use.

Standard Unix Mbox Spool File or Directory: To read and store e-mail in the mail spool on your local system, select this option. You need to provide the path to the mail spool you want to use.

None: If you do not plan to check e-mail with this account, select this option. There are no configuration options.

12.2.3.1 Configuration Options for IMAP+, POP, and USENET

If you selected IMAP +, POP, or USENET News as the server type, you need to specify additional information.

If you are not sure about the correct server address, user name or security setting, contact your system administrator or e-mail provider.

1. Type the host name of your e-mail server into the text box *Server*.

2. Type your user name for the account into the text box *Username*.

3. Choose a security setting supported by your mail server. For security reasons, avoid using *No Encryption*.

4. Select your authentication type in the *Authentication* list. To have Evolution check for supported authentication types, click *Check for Supported Types*. Then choose one of the options without a strikeout.
   Some servers do not announce the authentication mechanisms they support. Therefore clicking this button is not a guarantee that the shown mechanisms actually work.

5. Click *Continue*.

12.2.3.2 Configuration Options for Exchange Web Services

If you selected Exchange Web Services as the server type, you need to specify additional information.

If you are not sure about the correct server address, user name or security setting, contact your system administrator or e-mail provider.

1. Type your user name for the account into the text box *Username*.

2. Type the EWS URL of your e-mail server into the text box *Host URL*.
   If available, type the address of an Offline Address Book into the text box *OAB URL*.
   If your login name and the name of your mailbox differ, select *Open Mailbox of other user*. Then type the mailbox name into the text box below.

3. Select an authentication type in the *Authentication* list. To have Evolution check for supported authentication types, click *Check for Supported Types*. Then choose one of the options without a strikeout.
   Some servers do not announce the authentication mechanisms they support. Therefore clicking this button is not a guarantee that the shown mechanisms actually work.

4. Click *Continue*.

12.2.3.3   Local Configuration Options

If you selected *Local Delivery*, *MH-Format Mail Directories*, *Maildir-Format Mail Directories*, or *Standard Unix Mbox Spool File or Directory*, specify the path to the local files or directories in the path field.

12.2.4   Receiving Options

After you have selected a mail delivery mechanism, you can set some preferences for its behavior.

12.2.4.1   IMAP+ Receiving Options

If you selected IMAP+ as the receiving server type, you will now see a page of options to specify the behavior of Evolution.

1. You can choose from the following options:

   Check for new messages every ... minutes

   > Select if you want Evolution to automatically check for new mail. Set how often to check.

   Check for new message in all folders

   > Select if you want to check for new messages in all folders.

   Check for new message in subscribed folders

   > Select if you want to check for new messages in subscribed folders.

   Use Quick Resync if the server supports it

   > Select if you want to use Quick Resync which makes browsing mail faster on supported servers.

   Listen for server change notifications

   > Select if you want Evolution to listen for change notifications. If you activate this option, Evolution will show you mail as it arrives. Therefore, you can usually deactivate *Check for new messages every ... minutes*.

   Show only subscribed folders

   > Select if you want Evolution to show only subscribed folders.
   > You can unsubscribe from folders to cut down on the number of irrelevant folders shown in Evolution and to reduce the amount of mail that is downloaded.

   Apply filters to new messages in all folders

   > Select if you want to apply filters to new messages, and whether to do so in all folders or only in the Inbox folder.

   Check new messages for Junk contents

   > Select if you want to check new messages for junk content, and whether to do so in all folders or only in the Inbox folder.

   Automatically synchronize remote mail locally

   > Select this to download all your mail, so you can read it offline.

2. Click *Continue*.

12.2.4.2   POP Receiving Options

If you selected POP as the receiving server type, you will now see a page of options to specify the behavior of Evolution.

1. You can choose from the following options:

    Check for new messages every ... minutes

    >   Select if you want Evolution to automatically check for new mail. Set how often to check.

    Leave messages on server

    >   Select if you want leave your mail on the server or delete it on the server when you download it to your computer. You can also set a period of time for which the messages will be kept on the server after they were downloaded.

    Disable support for all POP3 extensions

    >   Disabling POP3 extensions can help with old or misconfigured servers. Select if you have trouble receiving mail.

2. Click *Continue.*

12.2.4.3   USENET News Receiving Options

If you selected USENET News as the receiving server type, you will now see a page of options to specify the behavior of Evolution.

1. You can choose from the following options:

    Check for new messages every ... minutes

    >   Select if you want Evolution to automatically check for new mail. Set how often to check.

    Apply filters to new messages in all folders

    >   Select if you want to apply filters to new messages.

    Show folders in short notations

    >   Abbreviate folder names, for example, `comp.os.linux` appears as `c.o.linux`.

In the subscription dialog, show relative folder names

> Display only the name of the folder. For example, the folder `evolution.mail` would appear as `evolution`.

2. Click *Continue*.

12.2.4.4 Exchange Web Services Receiving Options

If you selected Exchange Web Services as the receiving server type, you will now see a page of options to specify the behavior of Evolution.

1. You can choose from the following options:

   Check for new messages every ... minutes

   > Select if you want Evolution to automatically check for new mail. Set how often to check.

   Check for new message in all folders

   > Select if you want to check for new messages in all folders.

   Apply filters to new messages in all folders

   > Select if you want to apply filters to new messages.

   Check new messages for Junk contents

   > Select if you want to check new messages for junk content, and whether to do so in all folders or only in the Inbox folder.

   Automatically synchronize remote mail locally

   > Select this to download all your mail, so you can read it offline.

   Connection timeout (in seconds)

   > Set maximum time to wait for an answer from the server.

   Cache offline address book

   > If you provided an OAB URL in the prior step, you can select caching an address book. This will make the address book available when offline.

2. Click *Continue*.

12.2.4.5 Local Delivery Receiving Options

If you selected that you want to receive mail through Local Delivery, you will now see a page of options to specify the behavior of Evolution.

1. Select *Check for new messages every … minutes* if you want Evolution to automatically check for new mail. Set how often to check.

2. Click *Continue*.

12.2.4.6 MH-Format Mail Directories Receiving Options

If you selected that you want to receive mail through MH-Format Mail Directories, you will now see a page of options to specify the behavior of Evolution.

1. Select *Check for new messages every … minutes* if you want Evolution to automatically check for new mail. Set how often to check.
   Select *Use the .folders summary file* if you want to use the `.folders` summary file.

2. Click *Continue*.

12.2.4.7 Maildir-Format Mail Directories Receiving Options

If you selected that you want to receive mail through Maildir-Format Mail Directories, you will now see a page of options to specify the behavior of Evolution.

1. Select *Check for new messages every … minutes* if you want Evolution to automatically check for new mail. Set how often to check.
   Select *Apply filters to new messages in Inbox* if you want to apply filters to new messages.

2. Click *Continue*.

12.2.4.8 Standard Unix Mbox Spool or Directory Receiving Options

If you selected that you want to receive mail through a Unix mbox Spool File or Directories, you will now see a page of options to specify the behavior of Evolution.

1. Select *Check for new messages every ... minutes* if you want Evolution to automatically check for new mail. Set how often to check.

   Select *Apply filters to new messages in Inbox* if you want to apply filters to new messages.

2. Select *Store status headers in Elm/Pine/Mutt format* to store status headers in a way compatible with Elm, Pine, and Mutt.

3. Click *Continue.*

12.2.5   Sending Mail

Now that you have entered information about how you plan to receive mail, Evolution needs to know about how you want to send it. Usually, a separate server configuration is necessary for this. Otherwise, this page will be skipped.

Select a server type from the *Server Type* list.

The following server types are available:

Sendmail: Uses the Sendmail program to send mail from your system. Sendmail is more flexible, but is not as easy to configure, so you should select this option only if you know how to set up a Sendmail service.

SMTP: Sends mail using a separate mail server. This is the most common choice for sending mail. If you choose SMTP, there are additional configuration options.

PROCEDURE 12.1: SMTP CONFIGURATION

1. Type the host address in the *Server* field.

   If you are not sure what your host address is, contact your system administrator or e-mail provider.

2. Select if your server requires authentication.

   If you selected that your server requires authentication, you need to provide the following information:

   a. Choose a security setting supported by your mail server. For security reasons, avoid using *No Encryption.*

   b. Select your authentication type in the *Authentication* list.

      or

Click *Check for Supported Types* to have Evolution check for supported types. Then choose one of the options without a strikeout.

Some servers do not announce the authentication mechanisms they support. Therefore, clicking this button is not a guarantee that the shown mechanisms actually work.

c. Type your user name in the *Username* field.

3. Click *Continue*.

12.2.6   Final Steps

Now that you have finished the e-mail configuration process, you need to give the account a name. The name can be any name you prefer. Type your account name on the *Name* field. Then click *Continue*. Finally, click *Apply*.

Depending on your configuration, you may now be asked for your e-mail passwords and whether you want to save them or want to always enter them when starting Evolution.

The Evolution main window will then open for the first time.

12.3   Using Evolution

Now that the first-run configuration has finished, you are ready to begin using Evolution. This section sums up the most important parts of the user interface.

FIGURE 12.1: EVOLUTION WINDOW

Menu Bar

The menu bar gives you access to nearly all of the features of Evolution.

Folder List

The folder list gives you a list of the available folders for each account. To see the contents of a folder, click the folder name. The contents are displayed in the e-mail list.

Toolbar

The toolbar gives you fast and easy access to the frequently used features in each component.

Search Bar

The search bar lets you search for e-mails. You can filter e-mails, contacts, and calendar entries and tasks using different criteria: a label, a search term, and an account or folder. The Search bar can also save frequently used searches to a search folder.

Message List

The message list displays a list of e-mails that you have received. To view an e-mail in the preview pane, select the e-mail.

Shortcut Bar

The shortcut bar at the left lets you switch between folders and program components.

Statusbar

The statusbar periodically displays a message, or informs you about the progress of a task, such as sending e-mail.
On the far left, you will find the Online/Offline indicator. Click the Online/Offline indicator to switch between being using Evolution in online or offline mode.

Preview Pane

The preview pane displays the contents of the e-mails that are selected in the e-mail list.

12.3.1 The Menu Bar

The menu bar's contents always provide all the possible actions for any view of your data.

File: Anything related to a file or to the operations of the application usually falls under this menu, such as creating things, saving them to disk, printing them, and quitting the program itself.

Edit: Contains tools to edit text and most configuration options.

View: Allows configuring the appearance of Evolution.

Folder: Contains actions that can be performed on folders.

Message: Contains actions that can be applied to a message.

Search: Lets you search for messages, or phrases within a message. You can also see previous searches you have made.

Help: Opens the Evolution application help.

12.3.2 The Shortcut Bar

The shortcut bar is the column on the left side of the main window. At the top, there is a list of folders for the selected Evolution component. The buttons at the bottom are shortcuts to the individual components, such as Mail and Contacts.

The folder list organizes your e-mail, calendars, contact lists, and task lists in a tree. Most people find one to four folders at the base of the tree, depending on the component and their system configuration. Each Evolution component has at least one, called *On This Computer*, for local information. For example, the folder list for the e-mail component shows all your e-mail accounts, local folders, and search folders.

If you receive large amounts of e-mail, you need additional ways to organize it. In Evolution, you can create own e-mail folders, address books, calendars, task lists, or memo lists.

12.3.2.1 Creating a folder

To create a new folder:

1. Click *File > New > Mail Folder*.

2. Type the name of the folder in the *Folder Name* field.

3. Select the location of the new folder.

4. Click *Create*.

12.3.2.2 Folder Management

Right-click a folder or subfolder to display a menu with the following options:

Mark All Messages As Read: Marks all the messages in the folder as read.

New Folder: Creates a new folder or subfolder in the same location.

Copy Folder To: Copies the folder to a different location. When you select this item, Evolution offers a choice of locations to copy the folder to.

Move Folder To: Moves the folder to another location.

Delete: Deletes the folder and all contents.

Rename: Lets you change the name of the folder.

Refresh: Refreshes the folder.

Properties: Shows the number of total and unread messages in a folder.

You can also rearrange folders and messages by dragging and dropping them.

Any time new e-mail arrives in a e-mail folder, that folder label is displayed in bold text, along with the number of new messages in that folder.

12.3.3 Using E-Mail

The e-mail component of Evolution has the following standout features:

- It supports multiple e-mail sources from many protocols.

- It lets you guard your privacy with encryption.

- It can speedily handle large amounts of e-mail.

- Search folders allow you to come back to often-used searches.

Below is a summary of the user interface of the e-mail window.

Message List

> The message list displays all the e-mails that you have. This includes all your read and unread messages and e-mail that is flagged to be deleted. With the *Show* drop-down box above the message you can filter the message list view using predefined and custom labels.

Preview Pane

> This is where your e-mail is displayed.
>
> If you find the preview pane too small, you can resize the pane, enlarge the whole window, or double-click the message in the message list to have it open in a new window. To change the size of a pane, drag the divider between the two panes.
>
> As with folders, you can right-click messages in the message list and get a menu of possible actions. This includes moving or deleting them, creating filters or search folders based on them, and marking them as junk mail.
>
> Actions related to e-mail, like *Reply* and *Forward*, appear as buttons in the toolbar and are also located in the right-click menu.

Templates

> Evolution allows you to create and edit message templates that you can use at any time to send mail with the same pattern.

12.3.4 Calendaring

To begin using the calendar, click *Calendars* in the shortcut bar. By default, the calendar shows today's schedule on a ruled background. At the upper right, there is a Tasks list, where you can keep a list of tasks separate from your calendar appointments. Below that, there is a list for memos.

Appointment List

> The appointment list displays all your scheduled appointments.

Month Pane

> The month pane is a small view of a calendar month. You can also select a range of days in the month pane to display a custom range of days in the appointment list.

Tasks

> Tasks are distinct from appointments because they generally do not have times associated with them. You can see a larger view of your task list by clicking *Tasks* in the shortcut bar.

Memos

> Memos, like Tasks, do not have times associated with them. You can see a larger view of your Memo list by clicking *Memos* in the shortcut bar.

12.3.5 Managing Contacts

To use the contacts component, click *Contacts* in the shortcut bar. The Evolution contacts component can handle all of the functions of an address book or phone book.

It does, however, also do more than a paper book. To share your address book on a network, you can use LDAP directories. To create a new contact entry, right-click an e-mail address. You can also search contacts using the search bar.

By default, the display shows all your contacts in alphabetical order, in a card-based view. You can select other views from the *View* menu.

12.4 For More Information

Get more information about Evolution from the application help available via F1 .

Find more information on the project home page https://wiki.gnome.org/Apps/Evolution.

13 Passwords and Keys: Signing and Encrypting Data

The GNOME Passwords and Keys program is an important component of the encryption infrastructure on your system. With this program, you can create and manage PGP and SSH keys, import, export and share keys, back up your keys and keyring, and cache your passphrase.

Start the program by choosing *Applications › Utilities › Passwords and Keys*

FIGURE 13.1: PASSWORD AND KEYS MAIN WINDOW

13.1 Signing and Encryption

Signing. Attaching electronic signatures to pieces of information, such as e-mail messages or software to prove its origin. To keep someone else from writing messages using your name, and to protect both you and the people you send them to, you should sign your mails. Signatures help you check the sender of the messages you receive and distinguish authentic messages from malicious ones.

Software developers sign their software so that you can check the integrity. Even if you get the software from an unofficial server, you can verify the package with the signature.

Encryption. You might also have sensitive information you want to protect from other parties. Encryption helps you transform data and make it unreadable for others. This is important for companies so they can protect internal information and their employees' privacy.

13.2 Generating a New Key Pair

To exchange encrypted messages with other users, you must first generate your own pair of keys. It consists of two parts:

- **Public Key.** This key is used for encryption. Distribute it to your communication partners, so they can use it to encrypt files or messages for you.

- **Private Key.** This key is used for decryption. Use it to make encrypted files or messages from others (or yourself) legible again.

> **❗ Important: Access to the Private Key**
>
> If others gain access to your private key, they can decrypt files and messages intended only for you. Never grant others access to your private key.

13.2.1 Creating OpenPGP Keys

OpenPGP is a non-proprietary protocol for encrypting e-mail with the use of public-key cryptography based on PGP. It defines standard formats for encrypted messages, signatures, private keys, and certificates for exchanging public keys.

1. Click *Applications* > *Utilities* > *Passwords and Keys*.

2. Click *File* > *New*.

3. Select *PGP Key* and click *Continue*.

4. Specify your full name and e-mail address.

5. Click *Advanced key options* to specify the following advanced options for the key.

   Comment
   > An optional comment.

   Encryption Type
   > Specifies the encryption algorithms used to generate your keys. *DSA ElGamal* is the recommended choice because it lets you encrypt, decrypt, sign, and verify as needed. Both *DSA (sign only)* and *RSA (sign only)* allow only signing.

Key Strength

> Specifies the length of the key in bits. The longer the key, the more secure it is (provided a strong passphrase is used). Keep in mind that performing any operation with a longer key requires more time than it does with a shorter key. Acceptable values are between 1024 and 4096 bits. At least 2048 bits are recommended.

Expiration Date

> Specifies the date at which the key will cease to be usable for performing encryption or signing operations. You will need to either change the expiration date or generate a new key or subkey after this amount of time passes. Sign your new key with your old one before it expires to preserve your trust status.

6. Click *Create* to create the new key pair.
   The *Passphrase for New PGP Key* dialog opens.

7. Specify the passphrase twice for your new key, then click *OK*.
   When you specify a passphrase, use the same practices you use when you create a strong password.

13.2.2 Creating Secure Shell Keys

Secure Shell (SSH) is a method of logging in to a remote computer to execute commands on that machine. SSH keys are used in key-based authentication system as an alternative to the default password authentication system. With key-based authentication, there is no need to manually type a password to authenticate.

1. Click *Applications > Utilities > Passwords and Keys*.

2. Click *File > New*.

3. Select *Secure Shell Key*, then click *Continue*.

4. Specify a description of what the key is to be used for.
   You can use your e-mail address or any other reminder.

5. Optionally, click *Advanced key options* to specify the following advanced options for the key.

Encryption Type. Specifies the encryption algorithms used to generate your keys. Select *RSA* to use the Rivest-Shamir-Adleman (RSA) algorithm to create the SSH key. This is the preferred and more secure choice. Select *DSA* to use the Digital Signature Algorithm (DSA) to create the SSH key.

Key Strength. Specifies the length of the key in bits. The longer the key, the more secure it is (provided a strong passphrase is used). Keep in mind that performing any operation with a longer key requires more time than it does with a shorter key. Acceptable values are between 1024 and 4096 bits. At least 2048 bits is recommended.

6. Click *Just Create Key* to create the new key, or click *Create and Set Up* to create the key and set up another computer to use for authentication.

7. Specify the passphrase for your new key, click *OK*, then repeat.
   When you specify a passphrase, use the same practices you use when you create a strong password.

13.3   Modifying Key Properties

You can modify properties of existing OpenPGP or SSH keys.

13.3.1   Editing OpenPGP Key Properties

The descriptions in this section apply to all OpenPGP keys.

1. Click *Applications* › *Utilities* › *Passwords and Keys*.

2. Double-click the PGP key you want to view or edit.

3. Use the options on the *Owner* tab to add a photo to the key or to change the passphrase associated with the key.
   Photo IDs allow a key owner to embed one or more pictures of themselves in a key. These identities can be signed like normal user IDs. A photo ID must be in JPEG format. The recommended size is 120 × 150 pixels.
   If the chosen image does not meet the required file type or size, Passwords and Keys can resize and convert it on the fly from any image format supported by the GDK library.

4. Click the *Names and Signatures* tab to add a user ID to a key.
   See *Section 13.3.1.1, "Adding a User ID"* for more information.

5. Click the *Details* tab, which contains the following properties:

   Key ID: The Key ID is similar to the Fingerprint, but the Key ID contains only the last eight characters of the fingerprint. It is generally possible to identify a key with only the Key ID, but sometimes two keys might have the same Key ID.

   Type: Specifies the encryption algorithm used to generate a key. DSA keys can only sign. ElGamal keys are used to encrypt.

   Strength: Specifies the length, in bits, of the key. The longer the key, the more security it provides. However, a long key will not compensate for the use of a weak passphrase.

   Fingerprint: A unique string of characters that exactly identifies a key.

   Created: The date the key was created.

   Expires: The date the key can no longer be used (a key can no longer be used to perform key operations after it has expired). Changing a key's expiration date to a point in the future re-enables it. A good general practice is to have a master key that never expires and multiple subkeys that do expire and are signed by the master key.

   Override Owner Trust: Here you can set the level of trust in the owner of the key. Trust is an indication of how sure you are of a person's ability to correctly extend the Web of trust. When there is a key that you have not signed, the validity of the key is determined from its signatures and how much you trust the people who made those signatures.

   Export Complete Key: Exports the key to a file.

   Subkeys: See *Section 13.3.1.2, "Editing OpenPGP Subkey Properties"* for more information.

6. Click *Close*.

13.3.1.1 Adding a User ID

User IDs allow multiple identities and e-mail addresses to be used with the same key. Adding a user ID is useful, for example, when you want to have an identity for your job and one for your friends. They take the following form:

```
Name (comment) <e-mail address>
```

1. Click *Applications* > *Utilities* > *Passwords and Keys*.

2. Double-click the PGP key you want to view or edit.

3. Click the *Names and Signatures* tab, then click *Add Name*.

4. Specify a name in the *Full Name* field.
   You must enter at least five characters in this field.

5. Specify an e-mail address in the *E-Mail Address* field.
   Your e-mail address is how most people will locate your key on a key server or other key provider. Make sure it is correct before continuing.

6. In the *Key Comment* field, specify additional information that will display in the name of your new ID.
   This information can be searched for on key servers.

7. Click *Close*.

13.3.1.2   Editing OpenPGP Subkey Properties

Each OpenPGP key has a single master key used to sign only. Subkeys are used to encrypt and to sign as well. In this way, if your subkey is compromised, you do not need to revoke your master key.

1. Click *Applications* > *Utilities* > *Passwords and Keys*.

2. Double-click the PGP key you want to edit.

3. Click the *Details* tab, then click *Subkeys*.

4. Use the button to on the left of the dialog to add, delete, expire, or revoke subkeys.

Each subkey has the following information:

ID: The identifier of the subkey.

Type: Specifies the encryption algorithm used to generate a subkey. DSA keys can only sign, ElGamal keys are used to encrypt, and RSA keys are used to sign or to encrypt.

Created: Specifies the date the key was created.

Expires: Specifies the date the key can no longer be used.

Status: Specifies the status of the key.

Strength: Specifies the length, in bits, of the key. The longer the key, the more security it provides. However, a long key will not compensate for the use of a weak passphrase.

5. Click *Close*.

13.3.2   Editing Secure Shell Key Properties

The descriptions in this section apply to all SSH keys.

1. Click *Applications* › *Utilities* › *Passwords and Keys*.

2. Double-click the Secure Shell key you want to view or edit.

3. Use the options on the *Key* tab to change the name of the key or the passphrase associated with the key.

4. Click the *Details* tab, which contains the following properties:

Algorithm: Specifies the encryption algorithm used to generate a key.

Strength: Indicates the length in bits of a key. The longer the key, the more security it provides. However, a long key does not make up for the use of a weak passphrase.

Location: The location where the private key has been stored.

Fingerprint: A unique string of characters that exactly identifies a key.

Export Complete Key: Exports the key to a file.

5. Click *Close.*

13.4   Importing Keys

Keys can be exported to text files. These files contain human-readable text at the beginning and at the end of a key. This format is called an ASCII-armored key.

To import keys:

1. Click *Applications* › *Utilities* › *Passwords and Keys.*

2. Click *File* › *Import.*

3. Select a file containing at least one ASCII-armored public key.

4. Click *Open* to import the key.

You can also paste keys inside Passwords and Keys:

1. Select an ASCII-armored public block of text, then copy it to the clipboard.

2. Click *Applications* › *Utilities* › *Passwords and Keys.*

3. Click *Edit* › *Paste*

13.5   Exporting Keys

To export keys:

1. Click *Applications* › *Utilities* › *Passwords and Keys.*

2. Select the keys you want to export.

3. Click *File* › *Export.*

4. Specify a file name and location for the exported key.

5. Click *Save* to export the key.

You can also export keys to the clipboard in an ASCII-armored block of text:

1. Click *Applications* › *Utilities* › *Passwords and Keys*.

2. Select the keys you want to export.

3. Click *Edit* › *Copy*.

13.6 Signing a Key

Signing another person's key means that you are giving trust to that person. Before signing a key, carefully check the key's fingerprint to ensure that the key really belongs to that person.

Trust is an indication of how sure you are of a person's ability to correctly extend the Web of trust. When there is a key that you have not signed, the validity of the key is determined from its signatures and how much you trust the people who made those signatures.

1. Click *Applications* › *Utilities* › *Passwords and Keys*.

2. Select the key you want to sign from the *My Personal Keys* or *Other Keys* tabs.

3. Click *File* › *Sign*.

4. Select how carefully the key has been checked, then indicate if the signature should be local to your keyring, and if your signature can be revoked

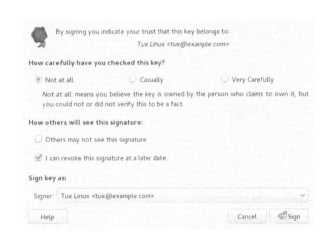

5. Click *Sign*.

13.7 Password Keyrings

You can use password keyring preferences to create or remove keyrings, to set the default keyring for application passwords or to change the unlock password of a keyring. To create a new keyring, follow these steps:

1. Click *Applications* › *Utilities* › *Passwords and Keys*.

2. Click *File* › *New* › *Password Keyring*, then click *Continue*.

3. Enter a new name for the keyring and click *Add*.

4. Set and confirm a new *Password* for the keyring and click *Create*.

To change the unlock password of an existing keyring, click the keyring in the *Passwords* tab and click *Change Password*. You need to provide the old password to be able to change it.

To change the default keyring for application passwords, click the keyring in the *Passwords* tab and click *Set as Default*.

13.8 Key Servers

You can keep your keys up-to-date by synchronizing keys periodically with remote keyservers. Synchronizing will ensure that you have the latest signatures made on all of your keys, so that the Web of trust will be effective.

1. Click *Applications* › *Utilities* › *Passwords and Keys*.

2. Click *Edit* › *Preferences*, then click the *Key Servers* tab.

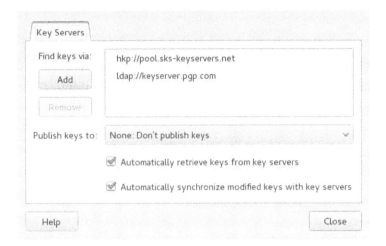

Passwords and Keys provides support for HKP and LDAP keyservers.

HKP Key Servers: HKP key servers are ordinary Web-based key servers, such as the popular `hkp://pgp.mit.edu:11371`, also accessible at http://pgp.mit.edu.

LDAP Key Servers: LDAP key servers are less common, but use the standard LDAP protocol to serve keys. ldap://keyserver.pgp.com is a good LDAP server.

You can *Add* or *Remove* key servers to be used using the buttons on the left. To add a new key server, set its type, host and port, if necessary.

3. Set whether you want to automatically publish your public keys and which keyserver to use. Set whether you want to automatically retrieve keys from key servers and whether to synchronize modified keys with keyservers.

4. Click *Close*.

13.9 Key Sharing

Key Sharing is provided by DNS-SD, also known as Bonjour or Rendezvous. Enabling key sharing adds the local Passwords and Keys users' public key rings to the remote search dialog. Using these local key servers is generally faster than accessing remote servers.

1. Click *Applications* › *Utilities* › *Passwords and Keys*.

2. Click *Edit* › *Preferences*, then click the *Key Servers* tab.

3. Select *Automatically synchronize modified keys with key servers.*

4. Click *Close.*

V Communication and Collaboration

14 Pidgin: Instant Messaging

Pidgin is an instant messaging (IM) client that allows you to connect to multiple accounts simultaneously. Chat live with your contacts in one tabbed interface, regardless of which IM system they use.

Pidgin supports the following instant messaging protocols: AOL* Instant Messenger (AIM), Bonjour, Gadu-Gadu, Google* Talk, GroupWise® Messenger, ICQ*, IRC, Jabber/XMPP, Microsoft Lync*/Office Communicator*, MSN* Messenger, MXit, MySpace* IM, QQ, SIMPLE, Yahoo!*, and Zephyr*. Pidgin supports many features of the various networks, such as file transfers, away messages, and typing notifications.

In the following, learn how to set up Pidgin and how to communicate with your contacts.

 Note: Pidgin May Not Be Installed

Before proceeding, make sure that the package `pidgin` is installed.

To chat with users of Microsoft Lync and Microsoft Office Communicator, make sure that the package `pidgin-sipe` is installed.

14.1 Starting Pidgin

To start Pidgin, select *Applications* › *Internet* › *Pidgin*.

14.2 Configuring Accounts

To use Pidgin, you must already have accounts on the systems you want to use. For example, to use Pidgin for your AIM account, you must first have an AIM account. Once you have those accounts, set them up in the Pidgin *Add Account* dialog.

PROCEDURE 14.1: ADDING AND EDITING ACCOUNTS

1. To start Pidgin, select *Applications* › *Internet* › *Pidgin*.

   If you start Pidgin for the first time, a message appears, prompting you to configure an account. Otherwise, Pidgin opens the Buddy List window, showing your contacts.

2. To add or edit an account from the Buddy List, select *Accounts* › *Manage Accounts*.

3. In the *Accounts* dialog, click *Add* to add a new account or select an existing account and click *Modify*.

4. On the *Basic* tab, select the protocol. The dialog to add or modify accounts differs for each protocol, depending on what setup options are available for that protocol.

5. Enter the data you received when you registered with the messaging service. This usually consists of the user name or e-mail address and a password.
   Your protocol might also support additional options, such as a buddy icon, alias, login options, or others.

6. Often the correct server data is now already set up. However, if you are configuring a Bonjour, Jabber, Groupwise, IRC, Microsoft Lync/Office Communicator, SIMPLE, or ZEPHYR account, you will need to add server or personal data.
   On the *Advanced* tab, enter the data you got from your system administrator or messaging service.

7. Click *Add* (new account) or *Save* (modified account).

8. Repeat this procedure to add accounts for each additional protocol you want to use.

After an account is added, you can log in to that account by entering your password in the Pidgin login dialog.

Use the *Accounts* menu to view and enable or disable accounts that you have configured.

14.3 Managing Contacts

Use the Buddy List to manage your contacts, also known as buddies. You can add and remove buddies from your Buddy List. You can also organize your buddies in groups, so they are easy to find.

After your accounts are set up, all buddies who are online appear in your Buddy List. If you want buddies who are not online to appear in the Buddy List, click *Buddies > Show > Offline Buddies*.

FIGURE 14.1: PIDGIN BUDDY LIST

To add a buddy to your Buddy List, click *Buddies > Add Buddy*, then enter the information about that buddy.

 ## Note: Adding Contacts for Certain Protocols

For some protocols, you cannot add a buddy in the Pidgin interface. You must use the official client for those protocols if you want to add to your buddy list. After you have added a buddy in the protocol's client, that buddy appears in your Buddy List.

To remove a buddy from the list of contacts, right-click the name of that buddy in the Buddy List and click *Remove*.

14.4 Chatting with Friends

It is necessary to be connected to the Internet to be able to chat with other participants. After a successful login, you are usually marked as *Available* in the Buddy List, and thus visible to others. To change your status, click the drop-down box at the bottom of the Buddy List and select another option.

To open a chat session, double-click a buddy name in the Buddy List. The Chat screen opens. Type your message, then press ⌈Enter⌋ to send.

If you open more than one chat session, the new session appears as a tab in the existing Chat window. To see all messages of a session and to be able to write a reply, click the tab of that session. To see multiple session side by side, use the mouse to drag a tab out of the window. A second window will open.

To close a chat session, close the tab or window for it.

FIGURE 14.2: PIDGIN CHAT SESSION

14.5 For More Information

This chapter explained the Pidgin options you need to know about to set up Pidgin and communicate with your contacts. It does not explain all of features and options of Pidgin. For more information, open Pidgin, then click *Help* › *Online Help* or press ⌈F1⌋.

For updates about new features and for the latest information, refer to the home page of the project at http://www.pidgin.im.

15 Ekiga: Using Voice over IP

Modern telecommunication entails more than making phone calls. It is also about text messaging and sometimes even video conferencing. Roaming enables you to be reachable under
one phone number all across the world. Ekiga brings these features to your Linux desktop, allowing you to communicate over broadband Internet.

 Note: Ekiga May Not Be Installed

Before proceeding, make sure that the package `ekiga` is installed.

Before starting, make sure that the following requirements are met:

* Your sound card is properly configured.

* A headset or a microphone and speakers are connected to your computer.

* For dialing in to regular phone networks, a SIP account is required. SIP (*Signaling protocol
  for Internet Telephony*) is the protocol used to establish sessions for audio and video conferencing or call forwarding.
  There are many VoIP providers all over the world. One provider is the Ekiga project itself,
  go to http://www.ekiga.net to learn more.

* For video conferencing: A Web cam is connected to your computer.

15.1 Starting Ekiga

Start Ekiga by clicking *Applications* › *Internet* › *Ekiga Softphone*.

15.2 Configuring Ekiga

On first start, Ekiga opens a configuration assistant that requests all data needed to configure
Ekiga. Proceed as follows:

1. Click *Forward*.

2. Enter your full name (name and surname). Click *Forward*.

3. Enter your `ekiga.net` account data or choose not to register with http://www.ekiga.net. Click *Forward*.
To add other accounts later, configure them using *Edit > Accounts*. Click *Forward*.

4. Enter your Ekiga Call Out Account data or choose not to register with http://www.ekiga.net. Click *Forward*.

5. Set your connection type and speed. Click *Forward*.

6. Choose the audio ringing, output and input device driver. In general, you can keep the *Default* setting. Click *Forward*.

7. Choose a video input device, if available. Click *Forward*.

8. Check the summary of your settings and apply them.

9. If registration fails after making changes to your configuration, restart Ekiga.

Ekiga allows you to maintain multiple accounts. To configure an additional account, proceed as follows:

1. Open *Edit > Accounts*.

2. Choose *Accounts > Add <account type>*. If you are unsure, select *Add a SIP Account*.

3. Enter the *Registrar* to which you have registered. This is usually an IP address or a host name that will be given to you by your Internet Telephony Service Provider. Enter *User*, and *Password* according to the data provided by your provider.

4. Leave the configuration dialog with *OK* and activate the account. The status of your account displayed in the Ekiga main window changes to *Registered*.

15.3   The Ekiga User Interface

The user interface has different modes. To switch between views, use the toolbar. The first mode is *Contacts*, the second is *Dialpad* and the last one is *Call History*. In addition, the *Call Panel* displays pictures and videos of local or remote Web cams.

By default, Ekiga opens in the *Contacts* mode. This view shows you a local address book lets you quickly open connections to often-used numbers.

Many of the functions of Ekiga are available with key combinations. *Table 15.1, "Key Combinations for Ekiga"* summarizes the most important ones.

TABLE 15.1: KEY COMBINATIONS FOR EKIGA

Key Combination	Description
Ctrl–O	Initiate a call with the current number.

Key Combination	Description
`Esc`	Hang up.
`Ctrl`-`N`	Add a contact to your address book.
`Ctrl`-`B`	Open the *Address Book* dialog.
`H`	Hold the current call.
`T`	Transfer the current call to another party.
`M`	Suspend the audio stream of the current call.
`P`	Suspend the video stream of the current call.
`Ctrl`-`W`	Close the Ekiga user interface.
`Ctrl`-`Q`	Quit Ekiga.
`Ctrl`-`E`	Start the account manager.
`Ctrl`-`J`	Activate *Call Panel* on the main user interface.
`Ctrl`-`+`	Zoom in to the picture from the Web cam.
`Ctrl`-`-`	Zoom out on the picture from the Web cam.
`Ctrl`-`0`	Return to the normal size of the Web cam display.
`F11`	Use full screen for the Web cam.

15.4 Making a Call

Once Ekiga is properly configured, making a call is easy.

1. Switch to the *Dialpad* mode.

2. Enter the SIP address of the party to call at the bottom of the window. The address should look like:

- for direct local calls: `sip:username@domainname` or `username@hostname`

- `sip:username@domainname` or `userid@sipserver`

3. Click *Call* or press `Ctrl`–`O` and wait for the other party to pick up the phone.

4. To end the call, click *Hang up* or press `Esc`.

If you need to tweak the sound parameters, click *Edit* › *Preferences*.

15.5 Answering a Call

Ekiga can receive calls in two different ways. First, can be called directly with `sip:user@host`, or via SIP provider. Most SIP providers enable you to receive calls from a normal land-line to your VoIP account. Depending on the mode in which you use Ekiga, there are several ways in which you are alerted to an incoming call:

Normal Application

Incoming calls can only be received and answered if Ekiga is already started. You can hear the ring sound on your headset or your speakers. If Ekiga is not started, the call cannot be received.

Panel Applet

Normally, the Ekiga panel applet runs silently without giving any notice of its existence. This changes when a call comes in. The main window of Ekiga opens and you hear a ringing sound on your headset or speakers.

Once you have noticed an incoming call, click *Accept* to answer the call then start talking. If you do not want to accept this call, click *Reject*. It is also possible to transfer the call to another SIP address.

15.6 Using the Address Book

Ekiga can manage your SIP contacts. All of the contacts are displayed in the *Contacts* tab, shown in the main window after start-up. To add a contact or a new contact group, run *Chat* › *Add Contact.*

If you want to add a new group, enter the group name into the bottom text box and press *Add*. The new group is then added to the group list and preselected.

The following entries are required for a valid contact:

Name

Enter the name of your contact. This may be a full name, but you can also use a nickname here.

Address

Enter a valid SIP address for your contact.

Groups

If you have many different contacts, add your own groups.

To call a contact from the address book, double-click the contact. The call is initiated immediately.

15.7 For More Information

The official home page of Ekiga is http://www.ekiga.org/. This site offers answers to frequently asked questions and more detailed documentation.

For information about the support of the H323 teleconferencing protocol in Linux, see http://www.voip-info.org/wiki/view/H.323. This is also a good starting point when searching for projects supporting VoIP.

To set up a private telephone network, you might be interested in the PBX software Asterisk http://www.asterisk.org/. Find information about it at http://www.voip-info.org/wiki-Asterisk.

VI Internet

16 Firefox: Browsing the Web

The Mozilla Firefox Web browser is included with SUSE® Linux Enterprise Desktop. With features like tabbed browsing, pop-up window blocking and download management, Firefox combines the latest browsing and security technologies with an easy-to-use interface. Firefox gives you easy access to different search engines to help you find the information you need.

16.1 Starting Firefox

To start Firefox, select *Applications > Internet > Firefox*.

16.2 Navigating Web Sites

The look and feel of Firefox is similar to that of other browsers. It is shown in *Figure 16.1, "The Browser Window of Firefox"*. The navigation toolbar includes *Forward* and *Back*, the location bar for a Web address, and the search bar. Bookmarks are also available for quick access from the bookmarks toolbar. For more information about the various Firefox features, use the *Help* menu in the menu bar.

 Note: Using the Menu Bar

While most functions of Firefox are available through the three-lines button (≡), some are only available from the menu bar.

The menu bar of Firefox is hidden by default. To temporarily show it, press Alt . It will then be displayed until you click elsewhere in the Firefox window.

To permanently enable the Firefox menu bar, first press Alt , then choose *View > Toolbars > Menu Bar*.

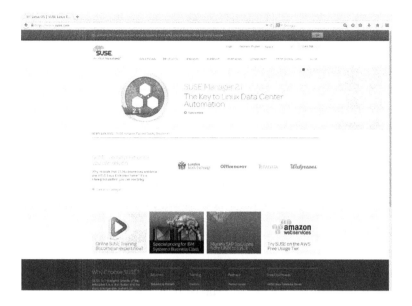

FIGURE 16.1: THE BROWSER WINDOW OF FIREFOX

16.2.1 The Location Bar

When typing into the location bar, an auto-completion drop-down box opens. It shows all previous location addresses and bookmarks containing the characters you type. The matching phrase is highlighted in bold. Entries visited most frequently and recently are listed first.

List entries from the bookmark list are marked with a star. Bookmarks with tags are marked with an additional label followed by the tag names. List entries from the browsing history are not marked. To search in your bookmarks only, type `*` as the first character of your search.

Use `↑` and `↓` or the mouse wheel to navigate the list. Press `Enter` or click an entry to go to the selected page. `Del` removes an entry from the list if it is an entry from the history. Bookmarked entries can only be removed by deleting the associated bookmark.

16.2.2 Zooming

Firefox offers two zooming options: page zoom, the default, and text zoom. Page view zooms the entire page as is, with all elements of a page, including graphics, expanding equally while text zoom only changes the text size.

To toggle between page and text zoom, from the menu bar, choose *View › Zoom › Zoom Text Only*. To zoom in or out either use the mouse wheel while holding the `Ctrl` key, or use `Ctrl`-`+` and `Ctrl`-`-`. Reset the zoom factor with `Ctrl`-`0`.

16.2.3   Tabbed Browsing

Tabbed browsing allows you to load multiple Web sites in a single window. To switch between pages in use, use the tabs at the top of the window. If you often use more than one Web page at a time, tabbed browsing makes it easier to switch between pages.

Opening tabs

> To open a new tab, from the menu bar, select *File › New Tab* or press `Ctrl`-`T`. This opens an empty tab in the Firefox window. To open a link on a Web page or a bookmark in a tab, middle-click it. Alternatively, right-click a link and select *Open Link in New Tab*. You may also open an address in the location bar in a new tab with a middle-click or by pressing `Ctrl`-`Enter`.

Closing Tabs

> Right-click a tab to open a context menu, giving you access to tab managing options such as closing, reloading, or bookmarking. To close a tab, you may also use `Ctrl`-`W` or click the close button. Any closed tab can be restored by choosing from the menu bar, *History › Recently Closed Tabs*. To reopen the last closed tab, either choose *Undo Close Tab* from the context menu or press `Ctrl`-`Shift`-`T`.

Sorting Tabs

> By default, tabs are sorted in the order you opened them. Rearrange the tab order by dragging and dropping a tab to the desired position. If you have opened a large number of tabs, they cannot all be displayed in the tab bar at the same time. Use the arrows at the ends of the bar to move left or right-click the down arrow at the right end of the tab bar to get a list of all tabs.

Dragging and Dropping

> Drag and drop also works with tabs. Drag a link onto an existing tab to open it in that tab or drag and drop a link on an empty space in the tab bar to open a new tab. Drag and drop a tab outside of the tab bar to open it in a new browser window.

16.2.4 Using the Sidebar

Use the left side of your browser window for viewing bookmarks or browsing history. Extensions may add new ways to use the sidebar as well. To display the sidebar, from the menu bar, select *View > Sidebar* and select the desired contents.

16.3 Finding Information

There are two ways to find information in Firefox: use the search bar to search the Internet with a search engine or the find bar to search the page currently displayed.

16.3.1 Finding Information on the Web

Firefox has a search bar that can access different engines like Google, Yahoo, or Amazon. For example, if you want to find information about SUSE using the current engine, click in the search bar, type SUSE, and press Enter. The results appear in your window.

To choose a different search engine, type your search term, then click one of the search provider icons at the bottom of the appearing pop-up.

16.3.1.1 Customizing the Search Bar

If you want to change the order, add, or delete a search engine, proceed as follows.

1. Click the icon to the left of the search bar.

2. From the pop-up, select *Change Search Settings*.

3. To delete an entry, click *Remove*. To change the order of entries, use the mouse to drag them.
   To add a search engine, click *Add More Search Engines*. Firefox displays a Web page with available search plug-ins. You can choose from Wikipedia, IMDB, Flickr, and numerous others. To install a search plug-in, click *Add to Firefox*.

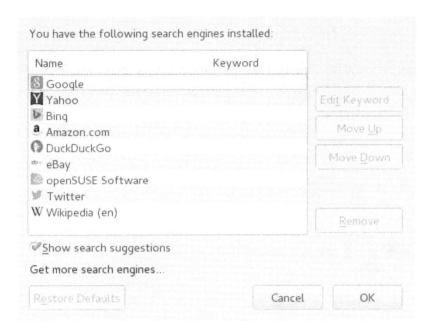

You have the following search engines installed:

Name	Keyword
Google	
Yahoo	
Bing	
Amazon.com	
DuckDuckGo	
eBay	
openSUSE Software	
Twitter	
Wikipedia (en)	

Edit Keyword

Move Up

Move Down

Remove

☑ Show search suggestions

Get more search engines...

Restore Defaults   Cancel   OK

FIGURE 16.2: MANAGE SEARCH ENGINES

Some Web sites offer search engines that you can add directly to the search bar. Whenever you are visiting such a Web site, the icon to the left of the search bar gains a + sign. Click the icon and select *Add.*

16.3.1.2   Adding Keywords to Your Online Searches

Firefox lets you define own *keywords*: abbreviations to use as a URL shortcut for a particular search engine. If you define ws as a keyword for the Wikipedia search for example, you can now type ws *SEARCHTERM* into the location bar to search Wikipedia for *SEARCHTERM*.

To assign a shortcut for a search engine from the search bar, click the icon to the left of the search bar. Then select *Change Search Settings.* Select a search engine, then double-click its *Keyword* column.

It is also possible to define a keyword for any search field on a Web site. Proceed as follows:

1. Right-click the search field and choose *Add a Keyword for this Search* from the menu that opens. The *Add Bookmark* dialog appears.

2. In *Name,* enter a descriptive name for this keyword.

3. Enter your *Keyword* for this search.

4. Choose the location where to save this keyword with *Create In*.

5. Finalize with *Add*.

 Tip: Keywords for Regular Web sites

Using keywords is not restricted to search engines. You can also add a keyword to a bookmark (via the bookmark's properties). For example, if you assign `suse` to the SUSE home page bookmark, you can open it by typing `suse` into the location bar.

16.3.2 Searching in the Current Page

To search inside a Web page, in the menu bar, click *Edit › Find in This Page* or press `Ctrl`–`F`. The find bar opens. It is usually displayed at the bottom of a window. Type your query in the text box. Firefox finds the first occurrence of this phrase as you type. You can find other occurrences of the phrase by pressing `F3` or the *Next* button in the find bar. Clicking the *Highlight All* button will highlight all occurrences of the phrase. Checking the *Match Case* option makes the query case-sensitive.

Firefox also offers two quick-find options. Click anywhere you like to start a search on a Web page, type the key `/` immediately followed by the search term. The first occurrence of the search term will be highlighted as you type. Use `F3` to find the next occurrence. It is also possible to limit quick-find to links only. This search option is available by typing the key `'`.

16.4 Managing Bookmarks

Bookmarks offer a convenient way of saving links to your favorite Web sites. Firefox not only makes it very easy to add new bookmarks with just one mouse click, it also offers multiple ways to manage large bookmark collections. You can sort bookmarks into folders, classify them with tags, or filter them with smart bookmark folders.

Add a bookmark by clicking the star in the location bar. The star will turn blue to indicate the page was bookmarked. The bookmark will be saved in the *Unsorted Bookmarks* folder under the page title. To change the name and folder of your bookmark or add tags, after bookmarking, click the star again. This will open a pop-up where you can make your changes.

To bookmark all open tabs, right-click in a tab and choose *Bookmark All Tabs*. Firefox asks you to create a new folder for the tab links.

To remove a bookmark, open the bookmarked location. Then, click the star and click *Remove Bookmark*.

16.4.1   Organizing Bookmarks

The *Library* can be used to manage the properties (name and address location) for each bookmark and organize the bookmarks into folders and sections. It resembles *Figure 16.3, "The Firefox Bookmark Library"*.

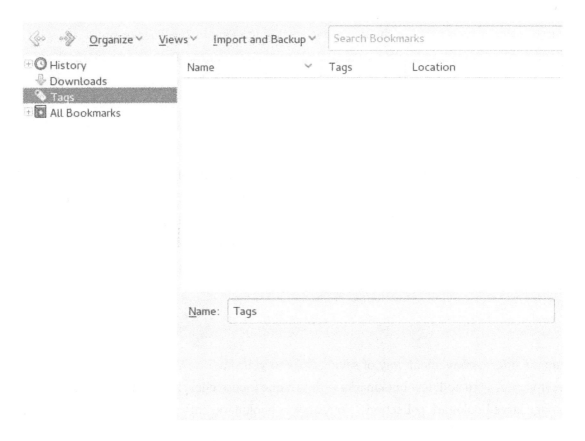

FIGURE 16.3: THE FIREFOX BOOKMARK LIBRARY

To open the *Library*, in the menu bar, click *Bookmarks › Show All Bookmarks*. The library window is split into two parts: the left pane shows the folder tree view, the right pane the subfolders and bookmarks of the selected folder. Use *Views* to customize the right pane. The left pane contains three main folders:

History

Contains your complete browsing history. You cannot alter this list other than by deleting entries from it.

Tags

Lists bookmarks for each tag you have specified. See *Section 16.4.2, "Tags"* for more information on tags.

All Bookmarks

This category contains the three main bookmark folders:

Bookmarks Toolbar

Contains the bookmarks and folders displayed beneath the location bar. See *Section 16.4.6, "The Bookmarks Toolbar"* for more information.

Bookmarks Menu

Holds the bookmarks and folder accessible via the *Bookmarks* entry in the main menu or the bookmarks side menu.

Unsorted Bookmarks

Contains all bookmarks created with a single click the star in the location bar. This folder is only visible in the library and the bookmarks sidebar.

Organize your bookmarks using the right pane. Choose actions for folders or bookmarks either from the context menu that opens when you right-click an item or from the *Organize* menu. The properties of a chosen folder or bookmark can be edited in the bottom part of the right pane. By default, only *Name, Location,* and *Tags* are displayed for a bookmark. Click the arrow next to *More* to gain access to all properties.

To rearrange your bookmarks, use the mouse to drag them. You can use this to move a bookmark or a folder to a different folder, or to change the order of bookmarks in a folder.

16.4.2 Tags

Tags offer a convenient way to file a bookmark under several categories. You can tag a bookmark with as many terms as you want. For example, to access all sites tagged with `suse`, enter `suse` into the location bar. For each tag, an item is automatically created in the `Recent Tags` folder of the library. Drag and drop an item for a tag onto the bookmark toolbar to easily access it.

To add tags to a bookmark, open the bookmark in Firefox and click the yellow star in the location bar. The *Edit This Bookmark* dialog opens where you can add a comma separated list of tags. It is also possible to add tags via the bookmark's properties dialog which you can open in the library or by right-clicking a bookmark in the menu or the toolbar.

16.4.3 Importing and Exporting Bookmarks

To import bookmarks from another browser or from a file in HTML format, open the library by choosing from the menu bar, *Bookmarks › Show All Bookmarks*. To start the Import Wizard, click *Import and Backup › Import Bookmarks from HTML* and choose an import location. Start the import by clicking *Next*. Imports from an HTML file are imported as is.

Exporting bookmarks is also done via *Import and Backup* in the library window. To save your bookmarks as an HTML file, choose *Export Boomarks to HTML*. To create a backup of your bookmarks, choose *Backup*. Firefox uses a JavaScript Object Notation file format (`.json`) for backups.

To restore a bookmark backup, click *Import and Backup › Restore*. Then locate the backup you want to restore from.

16.4.4 Live Bookmarks

Live Bookmarks display headlines in your bookmark menu and keep you up to date with the latest news. This enables you to save time with one glance at your favorite sites. Live bookmarks update automatically. Many sites and blogs support this format.

To create a Live Bookmark, look for orange buttons on Web sites that either read `RSS` or consist of a dot and three nested quarter circles. Click the icon. Usually, that will lead you to a page where all the headlines of the are displayed. On that page, choose *Subscribe Now*. A dialog opens in which to select the name and location of your live bookmark. Confirm with *Add*. This page also lets you choose alternative applications to subscribe with, such as *My Yahoo*.

16.4.5　Smart Bookmark Folders

Smart bookmark folders are virtual bookmark folders that are dynamically updated. There are three smart bookmark folders: The *Most Visited* links are available from your bookmarks toolbar. *Recently Bookmarked* links and *Recent Tags* are located in the bookmarks menu.

16.4.6　The Bookmarks Toolbar

The `Bookmarks Toolbar` is displayed beneath the location bar and lets you quickly access bookmarks. You can also add, organize, and edit bookmarks directly. By default, the `Bookmarks Toolbar` is populated with a predefined set of bookmarks organized into several folders (see *Figure 16.1, "The Browser Window of Firefox"*).

To manage the `Bookmarks Toolbar` you can use the library as described in *Section 16.4.1, "Organizing Bookmarks"*. Its content is located in the Folder *Bookmarks Toolbar*. It is also possible to manage the toolbar directly. To add a folder, bookmark, or separator, right-click an empty space in the toolbar and select the appropriate entry from the pop-up menu. To add the current page to the bar, click the icon of the Web page in the location bar and drag it to the desired position on the bookmarks toolbar. Hovering over an existing bookmark folder will automatically open it, enabling you to place the bookmark within this folder.

To manage a certain folder or bookmark, right-click it. A menu opens which lets you *Delete* it or change its *Properties*. To move or copy an entry, choose *Cut* or *Copy* and *Paste* it to the desired position.

16.5　Using the Download Manager

Keep track of your current and past downloads with the help of the download manager. To start the download manager, in the menu bar, click *Tools › Downloads*. While downloading a file, a progress bar indicates the download status. If necessary, pause the download and resume it later. To open a downloaded file with the associated application, click *Open*. To open the location to which the file was saved, choose *Open Containing Folder*. *Remove From List* only deletes the entry from the download manager, however, it does not delete the file from the hard disk.

By default, all files are downloaded to `~/Desktop`. To change this behavior, in the menu bar, click *Edit › Preferences*. Go to *General*. Under *Downloads*, either choose another location or *Always ask me where to save files*.

Tip: Resuming Downloads

If your browser crashes or is closed while downloading, all pending downloads will automatically be resumed in the background when starting Firefox the next time. A download that was paused before the browser was closed can manually be resumed via the download manager.

16.6 Security

Since browsing the Internet has become more risky, Firefox offers various measures to make browsing safer. It automatically checks whether you are trying to access a site known to contain harmful software (malware) or a site known to steal sensitive data (phishing) and stops you from entering these sites. The Instant Web Site ID lets you easily check a site's legitimacy, and a password manager and the pop-up blocker offer additional security. With Private Browsing, you can surf the Internet without Firefox recording data on your computer.

16.6.1 Instant Web Site ID

Firefox allows you to check the identity of a Web page with a single glance. The icon in the location bar next to the address indicates which identity information is available and whether communication is encrypted:

Gray Globe

The site does not provide any identity information and communication between Web server and browser is not encrypted. Do not exchange sensitive information with such sites.

Gray Triangle

This site is from a domain that has been verified by a certificate, so you can be sure that you are really connected to the very site it claims to be. However, the site tried to load additional elements, such as images or scripts over an insecure connection. Firefox has blocked these items. Therefore, the page can look broken.

Gray Padlock

This site is from a domain that has been verified by a certificate, so you can be sure that you are really connected to the very site it claims to be. Communication with a "gray-padlock" site is always encrypted.

Green Padlock

This site completely identifies itself by a certificate that ensures a site is owned by the person or organization it claims to be. This is especially important when exchanging very sensitive data (for example when doing money transactions over the Internet). In this case you can be sure to be on the Web site of your bank when it sends complete identity information. Communication with a "green-padlock" server is always encrypted.

To view detailed identity information, click the icon of the Web site in the location bar. In the opening pop-up, click *More Information* to open the Page Info Window. Here, you can view the site's certificate, the encryption level, and information about stored passwords and cookies.

With the *Permissions* view you can set per-site permissions for image loading, pop-ups, cookies and installation permissions. The *Media* view lists all images, background graphics and embedded objects from a site and displays further information on each item together with a preview. It also lets you save individual items.

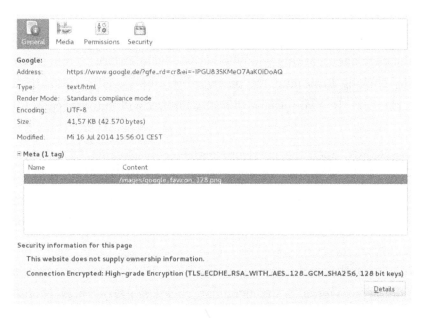

FIGURE 16.4: THE FIREFOX PAGE INFO WINDOW

16.6.2 Importing Certificates

Firefox comes with a certificate store for identifying certificate authorities (CA). Using these certificates enables the browser to automatically verify certificates issued by Web sites. If a Web site issues a certificate that has not been signed by one of the CAs from the certificate store, it is not trusted. This ensures that no spoofed certificates are accepted.

Large organizations usually use their own certificate authorities in-house and distribute the respective certificates via the system-wide certificate store located at `/etc/pki/nssdb`. To configure Firefox (and other Mozilla tools, such as Thunderbird) to use this system-wide CA store in addition to its own, export the `NSS_USE_SHARED_DB` variable. For example, you can add the following line to `~/.bashrc`:

```
export NSS_USE_SHARED_DB=1
```

Alternatively or additionally you can manually import certificates. To do so, in the menu bar, click *Advanced* › *Encryption* › *Your Certificates* in the *Preferences* dialog. Only import certificates you absolutely trust!

16.6.3   Password Management

Each time you enter a user name and a password on a Web site, Firefox offers to store this data. A pop-up at the top of the page opens, asking you whether you want Firefox to remember the password. If you accept by clicking *Remember*, the password will be stored on your hard disk in an encrypted format. The next time you access this site, Firefox will automatically fill in the login data.

To review or manage your passwords, open the password manager by clicking *Edit* › *Preferences* › *Security* › *Saved Passwords* in the menu bar. The password manager opens with a list of sites and their corresponding user names. By default, the passwords are not displayed. You can click *Show Passwords* to display them. Delete single or all entries from the list using *Remove* or *Remove All*, respectively.

To protect your passwords from unauthorized access, you can set a master password that is required when managing or adding passwords. In the menu bar, click *Edit* › *Preferences*, choose the category *Security* and activate *Use a Master Password*.

16.6.4   Private Browsing

By default, Firefox keeps track of your browsing history by storing content and links of visited Web sites, cookies, downloads, passwords, search terms and formula data. Collecting and storing this data makes browsing faster and more convenient. However, when you use a public terminal or a friend's computer, for example, you could turn this behavior off. In Private Browsing mode Firefox will not keep track of your browsing history nor will it cache the content of pages you have visited.

To enable the Private Browsing mode, in the menu bar, click *File › New Private Window*. The current Web site and all open tabs will be replaced by the Private Browsing information screen. As long as you will browse in private mode, the string `(Private Browsing)` will be displayed in the titlebar of the window.

Disable Private Browsing by closing the private window.

To make Private Browsing the default mode, open the *Privacy* tab in the Preference window as described in *Section 16.7.1, "Preferences"*, set *Firefox will:* to *Use custom settings for history* and then choose *Always use private browsing mode.*

 Warning: Bookmarks and Downloads

Downloads and bookmarks you made during Private Browsing mode will be kept.

16.7 Customizing Firefox

Firefox can be customized extensively.

- Change the way Firefox behaves by altering its preferences.

- Add functionality by installing extensions.

- Change the look and feel by installing themes.

To manage extensions, themes and plug-ins, Firefox has an add-on manager.

16.7.1 Preferences

Firefox offers a wide range of configuration options. These are available by choosing *Edit › Preferences* in the menu bar. Each option is described in detail in the online help, which can be accessed by clicking *Help* in the dialog.

FIGURE 16.5: THE PREFERENCES WINDOW

16.7.1.1   Session management

By default, Firefox automatically restores your session—windows and tabs— only after it has crashed, or after a restart because of an extension. However, it can be configured to restore a session every time it is started: Open the Preferences dialog as described in *Section 16.7.1, "Preferences"* and go to the category *General*. Set *When Firefox Starts:* to *Show My Windows and Tabs from Last Time*.

When you have multiple windows open they will only be restored the next time when you close all of them at once with *File › Quit* (from the menu bar) or with Ctrl–Q. If you close the windows one by one, only the last window will be restored.

16.7.1.2   Language Preferences for Web Sites

When sending a request to a Web server, the browser always sends the information about which language is preferred by the user. Web sites that are available in more than one language (and are configured to evaluate this language parameter) will display their pages in the language the browser requests. On SUSE Linux Enterprise Desktop, the preferred language is preconfigured to use the same language as the desktop. To change this setting, open the *Preferences* window as described in *Section 16.7.1, "Preferences"*, go to the category *Content* and *Choose* your preferred language.

16.7.1.3 Spell Checking

When typing into multiple-line text boxes, Firefox, by default, spell-checks what you type. Misspelled words are underlined in red. To correct a word, right-click it and select the correct spelling from the context menu. You may also add the word to the dictionary, if it is correct.

To change or add a dictionary, right-click anywhere in a multi-line text box and select the appropriate option from the context menu. Here you may also disable spell-checking for this text box. If you want to globally disable spell checking, open the *Preferences* window as described in *Section 16.7.1, "Preferences"* and go to the category *Advanced*. Uncheck *Check My Spelling As I Type*.

16.7.2 Add-ons

Extensions let you personalize Firefox to fit your needs. With extensions, you can change the look and feel of Firefox, enhance existing functionality, and add functions. For example, extensions can enhance the download manager, show the weather or control Web music players. Other extensions assist Web developers or increase security by blocking content such as ads or scripts.

There are thousands of extensions are available for Firefox. With the add-ons manager, you can install, enable, disable, update, and remove extensions.

If you do not like the standard look and feel of Firefox, install a new *theme*. Themes do not change the functionality, only the appearance of the browser.

16.7.2.1 Installing Add-ons

To add an extension or theme, start the add-ons manager with *Tools > Add-Ons* from the menu bar. It opens on the *Get Add-Ons* tab either displaying a choice of recommended add-ons or the results of your last search.

Use the *Search All Add-Ons* field to search for specific add-ons. Click an entry in the list to view a short description and a screenshot. Install the add-on by clicking *Add to Firefox* or open a Web page with detailed information by clicking the *Learn More* link.

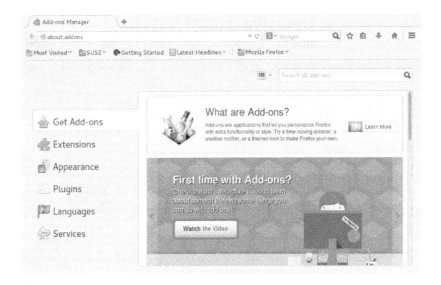

FIGURE 16.6: INSTALLING FIREFOX EXTENSIONS

If you want to browse all available add-ons or want to use advanced search options, click *See all ... results*. This opens the Firefox Add-ons Web page. To install an extension, click *Add to Firefox* on the description page of an extension.

To activate freshly installed extensions or themes, Firefox sometimes needs to be restarted by clicking *Restart now* in the add-ons manager. Restart this way to make sure that your browsing session will be restored.

16.7.2.2   Managing Add-ons

The Add-ons Manager also offers a convenient interface to manage extensions, themes, and plug-ins. *Extensions* can be enabled, disabled or uninstalled. If an extension is configurable, its configuration options can be accessed via the *Preferences* button. In the *Themes* tab you may *Uninstall* a theme, or activate a different theme by clicking *Use Theme*. Pending extension and theme installations are also listed. Select *Cancel* to stop the installation. Although you cannot install *Plug-Ins* as a user, you may disable or enable them with the Add-ons manager.

Some add-ons require you to restart the browser when you uninstall or disable them. In such cases, after clicking either of these actions, a *Restart now* link appears in the add-ons manager.

16.8 Printing from Firefox

Before you actually print a Web page, you can use the print preview function to control how the printed page will look like. From the menu bar, choose *File › Print Preview*. Configure paper size and orientation per printer with *File › Page Setup*.

To print a Web page either choose, from the menu bar, *File › Print* or press `Ctrl`–`P`. The Printer dialog opens. To print with the default options click *Print*.

The Printer dialog also offers extensive configuration options to fine-tune the printout. On the *General* tab, choose a printer, the range to print, the number of copies and the order. *Page Setup* lets you specify the number of pages per side, the scaling factor and paper source and type. If the printer supports it, you can also activate double-sided printing here. Control how frames, backgrounds, header and footer are printed on the *Options* tab. You may also specify *Job* options, such as printing at a specific time, and the *Image Quality* in this dialog.

16.9 Controlling Adobe Flash Player Settings

Adobe Flash Player is a software that extends browsers with the ability to display certain animations and applications.

You can control the settings of the Adobe Flash Player plug-in with a settings manager. To start the Adobe Flash Player Settings, choose *Applications › Internet › Adobe Flash Player*. The dialog allows you to define your preferences with regard to *Storage, Camera and Mic, Playback* and to change some advanced settings. For more information, refer to http://www.macromedia.com/support/documentation/en/flashplayer/help/settings_manager.html.

16.10 For More Information

Get more information about Firefox from the official help Web site available via `F1`. More useful information is available from the following links:

Support forum: http://support.mozilla.com/forum

Main Menu reference: http://support.mozilla.com/kb/Menu+reference

Preferences reference: http://support.mozilla.com/kb/Options+window

Keyboard shortcuts: http://support.mozilla.com/kb/Keyboard+shortcuts

17 gFTP: Transferring Data From the Internet

gFTP is a multithreaded file transfer client. It supports the FTP, FTPS (control connection only), HTTP, HTTPS, SSH, and FSP protocols. Furthermore, it allows the transfer of files between two remote FTP servers via FXP. To start gFTP, click *Applications › Internet › gFTP*.

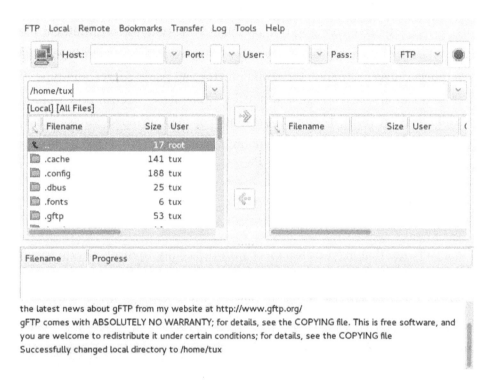

FIGURE 17.1: GFTP

17.1 ASCII vs. Binary Transfers

There are two common ways of transferring files via FTP: ASCII and binary. *ASCII* mode transfers files as text. ASCII files are `.txt`, `.asp`, `.html`, and `.php` files, for example. *Binary* mode transfers files as raw data. Binary files are `.wav`, `.jpg`, `.gif`, and `mp3` files, for example.

To change the transfer mode, click *FTP* and select *Binary* or *Ascii*.

When transferring ASCII files from Linux/Unix to Windows or vice versa, check the option *FTP › Preferences › FTP › Transfer Files in ASCII Mode* to ensure that newline characters are correctly converted. This option will automatically be disabled in Binary mode.

17.2   Connecting to a Remote Server

To connect to a remote server, do the following:

1. Click *Remote* › *Open Location*.

2. Specify a URL to connect to and click *Connect*.

3. Specify your user name and click *Connect*. Then specify your password and click *Connect*. To connect anonymously, leave the user name blank.

4. If the connection is successful, the right part of the gFTP window lists files from the remote computer. The file listing on the left side continues to show files from your local computer. You can now upload and download files via drag and drop or by using the arrow buttons.

To bookmark a site you access frequently, click *Bookmarks* › *Add Bookmark*. Specify a name for the bookmark, then click *Add*. The new bookmark is added to your list of bookmarks.

17.3   Transferring Files

In the following figure, the file list on the right contains the remote server's directory of files. The file list on the left side contains your local computer's directory of files (on your hard disk or network).

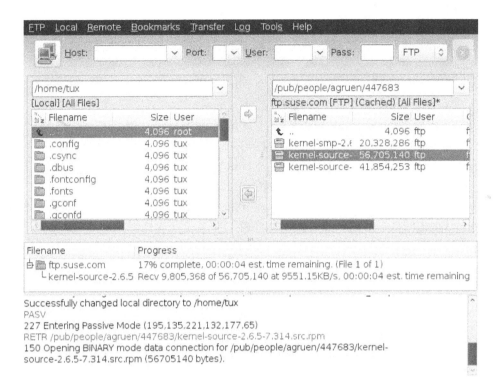

FTP Local Remote Bookmarks Transfer Log Tools Help

Host: ⌄ Port: ⌄ User: ⌄ Pass: FTP ⌄

/home/tux ⌄   /pub/people/agruen/447683 ⌄
[Local] [All Files]   ftp.suse.com [FTP] (Cached) [All Files]*

Filename   Size User   Filename   Size User
              4,096 root   ↖ ..   4,096 ftp
.config   4,096 tux   kernel-smp-2.(20,328,286 ftp
.csync   4,096 tux   kernel-source- 56,705,140 ftp
.dbus   4,096 tux   kernel-source- 41,854,253 ftp
.fontconfig   4,096 tux
.fonts   4,096 tux
.gconf   4,096 tux
.gconfd   4,096 tux

Filename   Progress
ftp.suse.com   17% complete, 00:00:04 est. time remaining. (File 1 of 1)
  └ kernel-source-2.6.5 Recv 9,805,368 of 56,705,140 at 9551.15KB/s, 00:00:04 est. time remaining

Successfully changed local directory to /home/tux
PASV
227 Entering Passive Mode (195,135,221,132,177,65)
RETR /pub/people/agruen/447683/kernel-source-2.6.5-7.314.src.rpm
150 Opening BINARY mode data connection for /pub/people/agruen/447683/kernel-source-2.6.5-7.314.src.rpm (56705140 bytes).

FIGURE 17.2: GFTP FILE TRANSFER

To download files, select the files you want to download in the remote list of files, then click the left arrow button. The progress of each download is listed in the field in the middle of the window. If the transfer is successful, the files appear in the directory listing on the left.

To upload a file, select the files you want to upload in your local directory listing on the left, then click the right arrow button. The progress of each download is listed in the field in the middle of the window. If the transfer is successful, the files appear in the remote directory listing on the right.

To modify preferences for your downloads, click *FTP* › *Preferences*.

17.4 Setting Up an HTTP Proxy Server

To set up an HTTP proxy server, do the following:

1. Click *FTP* › *Preferences*, then select the *FTP* tab.

2. Enter the *Proxy hostname* and *Proxy port*. If applicable, also provide your login credentials for the proxy server. Choose a proxy type from the *Proxy Server Type* drop-down box.

3. Click the *HTTP* tab, and enter the same proxy server information as above in the dialog. Note that port numbers for FTP and HTTP proxy may differ.

4. Click *OK*.

17.5 For More Information

You can find more information about gFTP at http://www.gftp.org.

VII Graphics

18 GIMP: Manipulating Graphics

GIMP (*the GNU Image Manipulation Program*) is a program for creating and editing raster graphics. In most aspects, its features are comparable to those of Adobe* Photoshop* and other commercial programs. Use it to resize and retouch photographs, design graphics for Web pages, create covers for your custom CDs, or almost any other graphics project. It meets the needs of both amateurs and professionals.

GIMP is an extremely complex program. Only a small range of features, tools, and menu items are discussed in this chapter. See *Section 18.8, "For More Information"* for ideas of where to find more information about the program.

18.1 Graphics Formats

There are two main types of digital graphics: raster and vector. GIMP is intended for working with raster graphics, which are most often used for digital photographs or scanned images.

Raster Images. A raster image is a collection of pixels: Small blocks of color that, when put together create an entire image. High resolution images contain a large number of pixels. Because of this, such image files can easily become quite large. It is not possible to increase the size of a raster image without losing quality.

GIMP supports most common formats of raster graphics, like JPEG, PNG, GIF, BMP, TIFF, PSD, and more.

Vector Images. Unlike raster images, vector images do not store information about individual pixels. Instead, they use geometric primitives such as points, lines, curves, and polygons. Vector images can be scaled very easily. Depending on their content, vector image files can both be very small or very large. However, their file size is usually independent of their display size.

The disadvantage of vector images is that they are not good at representing complex images with many different colors such as photographs. There are many specialized applications for vector graphics, for example Inkscape. GIMP has very limited support for vector graphics. For example, GIMP can open and rasterize vector graphics in SVG format or work with vector paths.

GIMP supports only the most common color spaces:

- RGB images with 8 bits per channel. This equals 24 bits per pixel in RGB images without an alpha channel (transparency). With an alpha channel, that equals 32 bits per pixel.

- Grayscale images with 8 bits per pixel.

- Indexed images with up to 255 colors

Many high-end digital cameras produce image files with color depths above 8 bits per channel. If you import such an image into GIMP, you will lose some color information. GIMP also does not support a CMYK color mode for professional printing.

18.2 Starting GIMP

To start GIMP, select *Applications* > *Graphics* > *GIMP*.

18.3 User Interface Overview

By default, GIMP shows three windows. The toolbox, an empty image window with the menu bar, and a window containing several docked dialogs. The windows can be arranged on the screen as you need them. If they are no longer needed, they can also be closed. Closing the image window when it is empty quits the application.

In the default configuration, GIMP saves your window layout when you quit. Dialogs left open reappear when you next start the program.

If you want to combine all windows of GIMP, activate *Windows* > *Single-Window Mode*.

18.3.1 The Image Window

Every new, opened, or scanned image appears in its own window. If there is more than one open image, each image has its own image window. There is always at least one image window open. If there is currently no image open, the image window is empty, containing only the menu bar and drop area, which can be used to open any file by dragging and dropping it there.

In Single-Window Mode, all image windows are accessible from a tab bar at the top of the window.

The menu bar at the top of the window provides access to all image functions. You can also access the menu by right-clicking the image or clicking the small arrow button in the top left corner of the rulers.

The *File* menu offers the standard file operations, such as *New, Open, Save, Print* and *Close. Quit* quits the application.

With the items in the *View* menu, control the display of the image and the image window. *New View* opens a second display window of the current image. Changes made in one view are reflected in all other views of that image. Alternate views are useful for magnifying a part of an image for manipulation while seeing the complete image in another view. Adjust the magnification level of the current window with *Zoom*. When *Fit Image in Window* is selected, the image window is resized to fit the current image display exactly.

18.3.2   The Toolbox

The toolbox contains drawing tools, a color selector and a freely configurable space for options pages. If you accidentally close the toolbox, you can reopen it by clicking *Tools > New Toolbox*.

To find out what a particular tool does, hover over its icon. At the very top, there is a drop area which can be used to open any image file by simply dragging and dropping it there.

FIGURE 18.1: THE TOOLBOX

The current foreground and background color are shown in two overlapping boxes. The default colors are black for the foreground and white for the background. Click the box to open a color selection dialog. Swap the foreground and background color with the bent arrow icon to the upper right of the boxes. Use the black and white icon to the lower left to reset the colors to the default.

Under the toolbox, a dialog shows options for the currently selected tool. If it is not visible, open it by double-clicking the icon of the tool in the toolbox.

18.3.3   Layers, Channels, Paths, Undo

Layers shows the different layers in the current image and can be used to manipulate the layers. Information is available in *Section 18.6.6, "Layers"*.

Channels shows the color channels of the current image can manipulate them.

Paths are a vector-based method of selecting parts of an image. They can also be used for drawing. *Paths* shows the paths available for an image and provides access to path functions. *Undo* shows a limited history of modifications made to the current image. Its use is described in *Section 18.6.5, "Undoing Mistakes"*.

18.4   Getting Started

Although GIMP can be a bit overwhelming for new users, most quickly find it easy to use after they work out a few basics. Crucial basic functions are creating, opening, and saving images.

18.4.1   Creating a New Image

1. To create a new image, select *File › New*. This opens a dialog in which you can make settings for the new image.

2. If desired, select a predefined setting called a *Template*.

 Note: Custom Templates

To create a custom template, select *Windows › Dockable Dialogs › Templates* and use the controls offered by the window that opens.

3. In the *Image Size* section, set the size of the image to create in pixels or another unit. Click the name of the unit to select another unit from the list of available units.

4. To set a different resolution, click *Advanced Options*, then change the value for *Resolution*. The default resolution of GIMP is usually 72 pixels per inch. This corresponds to a common screen display and is sufficient for most Web page graphics. For print images, use a higher resolution, such as 300 pixels per inch.

   In *Color space*, select whether the image should be in color (*RGB*) or *Grayscale*. For detailed information about image types, see *Section 18.6.7, "Image Modes"*.

   In *Fill With* select the color the image is filled with. You can choose between *Foreground Color* and *Background Color* set in the toolbox, *White* or *Transparency* for a transparent image. Transparency is represented by a gray checkerboard pattern.

5. When the settings meet your needs, click *OK*.

18.4.2 Opening an Existing Image

To open an existing image, select *File › Open*.

In the dialog that opens, select the desired file. Then click *Open* to open the selected image.

18.5 Saving and Exporting Images

GIMP makes a distinction between saving and exporting images.

Saving an Image. The image is stored with all its properties in a lossless format. This includes, for example, layer and path information. This means that repeatedly opening and saving the image will neither degrade its quality nor how well it can be edited.

To save an image, use *File › Save* or *File › Save as*. To be able to store all properties, only the native format of GIMP is allowed in this mode: the XCF format.

Exporting an image. The image is stored in a format in which some properties can be lost. For example, most image formats, do not support layers. When exporting, GIMP will often tell you which properties will be lost and ask you to decide how to proceed.

To export an image, use *File › Overwrite* or *File › Export As*. Below is a selection of the most common file formats that GIMP can export to:

JPEG

> A common format for photographs and Web page graphics without transparency. Its compression method enables reduction of file sizes, but information is lost when compressing. It may be a good idea to use the preview option when adjusting the compression level. Levels of 85% to 75% often result in an acceptable image quality with reasonable compression. Repeatedly opening a JPEG and then saving can quickly result in poor image quality.

GIF

> Although very popular in the past for graphics with transparency, GIF is less often used now. GIF is also used for animated images. The format can only save *indexed* images. See *Section 18.6.7, "Image Modes"* for information about indexed images. The file size can often be quite small if only a few colors are used.

PNG

> With its support for transparency, lossless compression and good browser support, PNG is the preferred format for Web graphics with transparency. An added advantage is that PNG offers partial transparency, which is not offered by GIF. This enables smoother transitions from colored areas to transparent areas (*antialiasing*). It also supports the full RGB color space which makes it usable for photos. However, it cannot be used for animations.

18.6 Editing Images

GIMP provides a number of tools for making changes to images. The functions described here are those most interesting for smaller edits.

18.6.1 Changing the Size of an Image

After an image is scanned or a digital photograph is loaded from the camera, it is often necessary to modify the size for display on a Web page or for printing. Images can easily be made smaller either by scaling them down or by cutting off parts of them.

Enlarging an image is much more problematic. Because of the nature of raster graphics, quality is lost when an image is enlarged. It is recommended to keep a copy of your original image before scaling or cropping.

18.6.1.1   Cropping an Image

1. Select the crop tool from the toolbox (the paper knife icon) or click *Tools › Transform Tools › Crop*.

2. Click a starting corner and drag to outline the area to keep. A rectangle showing the crop area will appear.

3. To adjust the size of the rectangle, move your mouse pointer above any of the rectangle's sides or corners, then click and drag to resize as desired. If you want to adjust both width and height of the rectangle, use a corner. To adjust only one dimension, use a side. To move the whole rectangle to a different position without resizing, click anywhere near its center and drag to the desired position.

4. When you are satisfied with the crop area, click anywhere inside to crop the image or press `Enter`. To cancel the cropping, click anywhere outside the crop area.

18.6.1.2   Scaling an Image

1. Select *Image › Scale Image* to change the overall size of an image.

2. Select the new size by entering it in *Width* or *Height*.
   To change the proportions of the image when scaling (this distorts the image), click the chain icon to the right of the fields to break the link between them. When those fields are linked, all values are changed proportionately. Adjust the resolution with *X resolution* and *Y resolution*.
   The *Interpolation* option controls the quality of the resulting image. The default *Cubic* interpolation method usually is a good standard to use.

3. When you are finished, click *Scale*.

18.6.1.3 Changing the Canvas Size

The canvas is the entire visible area an image. Canvas and image are independent from each other. If the canvas is smaller than the image, you can only see part of the image. If the canvas is larger, you see the original image with extra space around it.

1. Select *Image* › *Canvas Size*.

2. In the dialog that opens, enter the new size. To make sure the dimensions of the image stay the same, click the chain icon.

3. After adjusting the size, determine how the existing image should be positioned in comparison to the new size. Use the *Offset* values or drag the box inside the frame at the bottom.

4. When you are finished, click *Resize*.

18.6.2 Selecting Parts of Images

It is often useful to perform an image operation on only part of an image. To do this, the part of the image with which you want to work must be selected. Areas can be selected using the selection tools available in the toolbox, using the quick mask, or combining different options. Selections can also be modified with the items under *Select*. The selection is outlined with a dashed line, called *marching ants*.

18.6.2.1 Using the Selection Tools

The main selection tools are easy to use. The more complicated paths tool is not described here.

To determine whether a new selection should replace, be added to, be subtracted from, or intersect with an existing selection, use the *Mode* row in the tool options.

Rectangle Select
> This tool can be used to select rectangular or square areas. To select an area with a fixed aspect ratio, width, height or size, activate the *Fixed* option and choose the relevant mode in the *Tool Options* dialog. To create a square, hold `Shift` while selecting a region.

Ellipse Select

Use this to select elliptical or circular areas. The same options are available as with the rectangular selection. To create a circle, hold `Shift` while selecting a region.

Free Select (Lasso)

With this tool, you can create a selection based on a combination of freehand drawing and polygonal segments. To draw a freehand line, drag the mouse over the image with the left mouse button pressed. To create a polygonal segment, release the mouse button where the segment should start and press it again where the segment should end. To complete the selection, hover the pointer above the starting point and click inside the circle.

Fuzzy Select (Magic Wand)

This tool selects a continuous region based on color similarities. Set the maximum difference between colors in the tool options dialog in *Threshold*. By default, the selection is based only on the active layer. To base the selection on all visible layers, check *Sample merged*.

Select by Color

With this tool, select all the pixels in the image with the same or a similar color as the clicked pixel. The maximum difference between colors can be set in the tool options dialog in *Threshold*. The important difference between this tool and Fuzzy Select is that Fuzzy Select works on continuous color areas while Select by Color selects all pixels with similar colors in the whole image regardless of their position.

Scissors

Click a series of points in the image. As you click, the points are connected based on color differences. Click the first point to close the area. Convert it to a regular selection by clicking inside it.

Foreground Selection

The Foreground Selection tool lets you semi-automatically select an object in a photograph with minimal manual effort.

To use the Foreground Selection tool, follow these steps:

1. Activate the Foreground Selection tool by clicking its icon in the Toolbox or choosing *Tools > Selection Tools > Foreground Select* from the menu.

2. Roughly select the foreground object you want to extract. Select as little as possible from the background but include the whole object. At this point, the tool works like the Fuzzy Select tool.

   When you release the mouse button, the deselected part of the image is covered with a dark blue mask.

3. Draw a continuous line through the foreground object going over colors which will be kept for the extraction. Do not paint over background pixels.

   When you release the mouse button, the entire background is covered with a dark blue mask. If parts of the object are also masked, paint over them. The mask will adapt.

4. When you are satisfied with the mask, press Enter. The mask will be converted to a new selection.

18.6.2.2   Using the Quick Mask

The quick mask is a way of selecting parts of an image using the paint tools. A good way to use it is to first create a rough selection using the Scissors or Free Select tool. Then start using the Quick Mask:

1. To activate the Quick Mask, in the lower left corner of the image window, click the icon with the dashed box. The Quick Mask icon now changes to a red box.

   The Quick Mask highlights the deselected parts of the image with a red overlay. Areas appearing in their normal color are selected.

    Note: Changing the Color of the Mask

   To use a different color for displaying the quick mask, right-click the quick mask button then select *Configure Color and Opacity* from the menu. Click the colored box in the dialog that opens to select a new color.

2. To modify the selection, use the paint tools.

   Painting with white selects the painted pixels. Painting with black deselects pixels. Shades of gray (colors are treated as shades of gray) create a partial selection. Partial selections allow a smooth transition between selected and deselected areas.

3. When you are finished, return to the normal selection view, by clicking the icon in the lower left corner of the image window. The selection is then displayed with the marching ants.

18.6.3 Applying and Removing Color

Most image editing involves applying or removing color. By selecting a part of the image, you can limit where color can be applied or removed. When you select a tool and move the mouse pointer onto an image, the appearance of the mouse pointer changes to reflect the chosen tool.

With many tools, an icon of the current tool is shown along with the arrow. For paint tools, an outline of the current brush is shown, allowing you to see exactly where you will be painting in the image and how large of an area will be painted.

18.6.3.1 Selecting Colors

The GIMP toolbox always shows two color swatches. The foreground color is used by the paint tools. The background color is used much more rarely, but it can easily be switched to become the foreground color.

1. To change the color displayed in a swatch, click the swatch. A dialog with five tabs opens.

2. These tabs provide different color selection methods. Only the first tab, shown in *Figure 18.2, "The Basic Color Selector Dialog"*, is described here. The new color is shown in *Current*. The previous color is shown in *Old*.

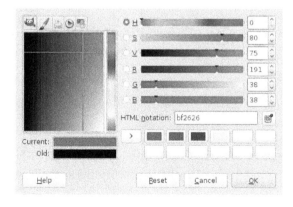

FIGURE 18.2: THE BASIC COLOR SELECTOR DIALOG

The easiest way to select a color is by using the colored areas in the boxes to the left. In the narrow vertical bar, click a color similar to the desired color. The larger box to the left then shows available nuances. Click the desired color. It is then shown in *Current*.

The arrow button to the right of *Current* allows saving colors. Click the arrow to copy the current color to the history. A color can then be selected by clicking it in the history.

A color can also be selected by directly entering its hexadecimal color code in *HTML Notation*.

The color selector defaults to selecting a color by hue. To select by saturation, value, red, green, or blue, select the corresponding radio button to the right. The sliders and number fields can also be used to modify the currently selected color. Experiment a bit to find out what works best for you.

3. When you are finished, click *OK*.

To select a color that already exists in your image, use the eye dropper tool. With the tool options, set whether the foreground or background color should be selected.

18.6.3.2   Painting and Erasing

To paint and erase, use the tools from the toolbox. There are a number of options available to fine-tune each tool. Pressure sensitivity options apply only when a pressure-sensitive graphics tablet is used.

The pencil, brush, airbrush, and eraser work much like their real-life equivalents. The ink tool works like a calligraphy pen. Paint by clicking and dragging. The bucket fill is a method of coloring areas of an image. It fills based on color boundaries in the image. Adjusting the threshold modifies its sensitivity to color changes.

18.6.3.3   Adding Text

To add text, use the text tool. Use the tool options to select the desired font and text properties. Click into the image, then start writing.

The text tool creates text in a special layer. To work with the image after adding text, read *Section 18.6.6, "Layers"*. When the text layer is active, it is possible to modify the text by clicking in the image to reopen the entry dialog.

18.6.3.4 Retouching Images—The Clone Tool

The clone tool is ideal for retouching images. It enables you to paint in an image using information from another part of the image. If desired, it can instead take information from a pattern.

When retouching, use a small brush with soft edges. In this way, the modifications can blend better with the original image.

To select the source point in the image, press and hold `Ctrl` while clicking the desired source point. Then paint with the tool. When you move the cursor while painting, the source point, marked by a cross, moves as well.

If the *Alignment* is set to *None* (the default setting), the source resets to the original when you release the left mouse button.

18.6.4 Adjusting Color Levels

Images often need a little adjusting to get ideal print or display results.

1. Select *Colors* › *Levels*. A dialog opens for controlling the levels in the image.

2. Good results can usually be obtained by clicking *Auto*. To make manual adjustments to all channels, use the dropper tools in *All Channels* to pick areas in the image that should be black, neutral gray, and white.
   To modify an individual channel, select the desired channel in *Channel*. Then drag the black, white, and middle markers in the slider in *Input Levels*. You can also use the dropper tools to select points in the image that should serve as the white, black, and gray points for that channel.
   If *Preview* is checked, the image window shows a preview of the image with the modifications applied.

3. When you are finished, click *OK*.

18.6.5 Undoing Mistakes

Most modifications made in GIMP can be undone. To view a history of modifications, use the undo dialog included in the default window layout or open one from the image window menu with *Windows* › *Dockable Dialogs* › *Undo History*.

The dialog shows a base image and a series of editing changes that can be undone. Use the buttons to undo and redo changes. In this way, you can often work back to the base image.

You can also undo and redo changes using *Undo* and *Redo* from the *Edit* menu. Alternatively, use the shortcuts `Ctrl`-`Z` and `Ctrl`-`Y`.

18.6.6 Layers

Layers are a very important aspect of GIMP. By drawing parts of your image on separate layers, you can change, move, or delete those parts without damaging the rest of the image.

To understand how layers work, imagine an image created from a stack of transparent sheets. Different parts of the image are drawn on different sheets. The stack can be arranged and sorted. Individual layers or groups of layers can shift position, moving sections of the image to other locations. New sheets can be added and others can be set removed or made invisible.

Use the *Layers* dialog to view the available layers of an image. The text tool automatically creates special text layers when used. The active layer is highlighted. The buttons at the bottom of the dialog offer several functions. More are available in the menu opened when a layer is right-clicked in the dialog. The two icon spaces before the image name are used for toggling image visibility (eye icon when visible) and for linking layers. Linked layers are marked with the chain icon and moved as a group.

18.6.7 Image Modes

GIMP has three image modes:

- RGB is a normal color mode and is the best mode for editing most images.

- Grayscale is used for black-and-white images.

- Indexed mode limits the colors in the image to a set number. The maximum number of colors in this mode is 255. It is mainly used for GIF images.

If you need an indexed image, it is normally best to edit the image in RGB, then convert to indexed right before exporting. If you export to a format that requires an indexed image, GIMP offers to index the image when exporting.

18.6.8   Special Effects

GIMP includes a wide range of filters and scripts for enhancing images, adding special effects to them or making artistic manipulations. They are available in *Filters*. Experimenting is the best way to find out what is available.

18.7   Printing Images

To print an image, select *File › Print* from the image menu. If your printer is configured in the system, it should appear in the list. You can configure printing options on *Page Setup* and *Image Settings* tabs.

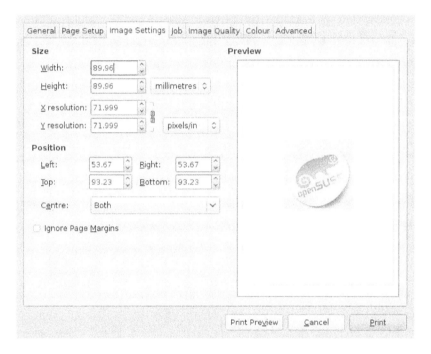

FIGURE 18.3: THE PRINT DIALOG

When you are satisfied with the settings, click *Print. Cancel* aborts printing.

18.8   For More Information

The following resources are very useful for users of GIMP. They contain much more information about GIMP than this chapter. If you want to use GIMP for more advanced tasks, you should not miss these resources.

- http://www.gimp.org is the official home page of The GIMP. News about GIMP and related software are regularly posted on the front page.

- *Help* provides access to the internal help system including the extensive GIMP User Manual. The package `gimp-help` needs to be installed. This documentation is also available online in HTML and PDF formats at http://docs.gimp.org. Translations into many languages are available.

- A collection of many interesting GIMP tutorials is maintained at http://www.gimp.org/tutorials/. It contains basic tutorials for beginners and tutorials for advanced or expert users.

- Printed books about GIMP are published regularly. You will find a selection of the best ones with short annotations at http://www.gimp.org/books/.

- GIMP functionality can be extended with scripts and plug-ins. Many such scripts and plug-ins are distributed in the GIMP package, but others can be downloaded from the Internet. At http://registry.gimp.org/, you will find a database of GIMP scripts and plug-ins.

You can also use mailing lists or IRC channels to ask questions about GIMP. Always try to find answers in the documentation mentioned above or in mailing list archives before asking your question. The time of experienced users present on GIMP lists and channels is limited. Be polite and patient. It may take some time before your question is answered.

- There are several mailing lists about GIMP. You will find them at http://www.gimp.org/mail_lists.html. The GIMP User list is the most appropriate place to ask user questions.

- There is a whole IRC network dedicated to GIMP and GNOME desktop environment— GIMPNet. You can connect to GIMPNet with your favorite IRC client by pointing it at the irc.gimp.org server. The #gimp-users channel is the right place to ask question about using GIMP. If you want to listen to developer's discussions, join the #gimp channel.

VIII Multimedia

19 GNOME Videos

GNOME Videos is the default movie player. GNOME Videos provides the following multimedia features:

- Support for a variety of video and audio files

- A variety of zoom levels and aspect ratios, and a full screen view

- Seek and volume controls

- Playlists

- Complete keyboard navigation

To start GNOME Videos, click *Applications* › *Sound & Video* › *Videos*.

19.1 Using GNOME Videos

When you start GNOME Videos, the following window is displayed.

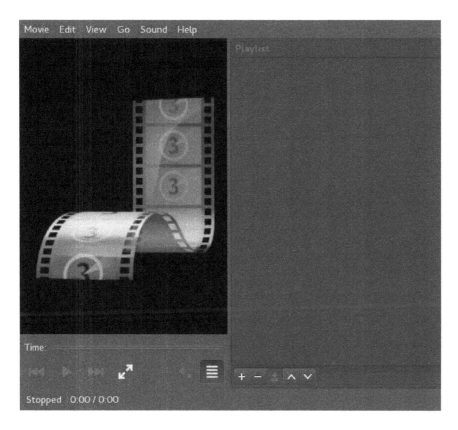

FIGURE 19.1: GNOME VIDEOS START-UP WINDOW

19.1.1 Opening a Video or Audio File

1. Click *Videos* > *Open*.

2. Select the files you want to open, then click *Add*

You can also drag a file from another application (such as a file manager) to the GNOME Videos window. GNOME Videos opens the file and plays the movie or song. GNOME Videos displays the title of the movie or song beneath the display area and in the titlebar of the window.

 Note: Unrecognized File Format

If you try to open a file format that GNOME Videos does not recognize, the application displays an error message and recommends a suitable codec.

You can double-click a video or audio file in GNOME Files to open it in the GNOME Videos window by default.

19.1.2   Opening a Video or Audio File By URI Location

1. Click *Videos* › *Open Location*.

2. Specify the URI location of the file you want to open, then click *Open*.

19.1.3   Playing a DVD, VCD, or CD

To play a DVD, VCD, or CD, insert the disc in the optical device of your computer, then click *Movie* › *Play Disc*.

To eject a DVD, VCD, or CD, click *Movie* › *Eject*.

To pause a movie or song that is playing, click the ▮▮ button, or click *Movie* › *Play/Pause*. When you pause a movie or song, the statusbar displays *Paused* and the time elapsed on the current movie or song.

To resume playing a movie or song, click the ▶ button, or click *Movie* › *Play/Pause*.

To play or pause a movie, you can also press P .

To view properties of a movie or song, click *View* › *Sidebar* to make the sidebar appear. The dialog contains the title, artist, year, and duration of movie or song, video dimensions, codec, frame rate, and the audio bit rate.

19.1.4   Seeking Through Movies or Songs

To seek through movies or songs, use any of the following methods:

To skip forward

Click *Go* › *Skip Forward*. Alternatively, use ← .

To skip backward

Click *Go* › *Skip Backward*. Alternatively, use → .

To move to next movie or song

Click *Go* › *Next Chapter/Movie*, or click the ▶▶ button.

To move to previous movie or song

Click *Go* › *Previous Chapter/Movie*, or click the ⏮ button.

19.1.5 Changing the Zoom Factor

To change the zoom factor of the display area, use any of the following methods:

To zoom to full screen mode

Click *View* › *Fullscreen*. Alternatively, press F .
To exit fullscreen mode, click *Leave Fullscreen* or press Esc .

To zoom to half size (50%) of the original movie or visualization

Click *View* › *Fit Window to Movie* › *Resize 1:2*.

To zoom to size (100%) of the original movie or visualization

Click *View* › *Fit Window to Movie* › *Resize 1:1*.

To zoom to double size (200%) of the original movie or visualization

Click *View* › *Fit Window to Movie* › *Resize 2:1*.

To switch between different aspect ratios, click *View* › *Aspect Ratio*.

The default aspect ratio is *Auto*.

19.1.6 Showing or Hiding Controls

To hide the window controls of GNOME Videos, click *View* › *Show Controls* and deselect the option. To show the controls on the GNOME Videos window, right-click the window, then select *Show Controls*. If the Show Controls option is selected, GNOME Videos shows the menubar, time elapsed slider, seek control buttons, volume slider, and statusbar on the window. If the Show Controls option is not selected, the application hides these controls and shows only the display area.

19.1.7 Managing Playlists

To show the playlist, click *View* › *Sidebar*. The Playlist sidebar is displayed.

You can use the Playlist dialog to do the following:

- **To add a track or movie:** Click the *Add* button. Select the file you want to add to the playlist, then click *OK*.

- **To remove a track or movie:** Select the file names from the file name list box, then click *Remove*.

- **To save a playlist to file:** Click the *Save Playlist* button, then specify a file name.

- **To move a track or movie up the playlist:** Select the file name from the file name list box, then click the *Move Up* button.

- **To move a track or movie down the playlist:** Select the file name from the file name list box, then click the *Move Down* button.

To hide the playlist, click *View > Sidebar*, or click the *Sidebar* button.

To enable or disable repeat mode, click *Edit > Repeat Mode*. To enable or disable shuffle mode, click *Edit > Shuffle Mode*.

19.1.8   Choosing Subtitles

To choose the language of the subtitles, click *View > Subtitles > Select Text Subtitles*, then select the subtitles language (DVD) or subtitle file (AVI etc.) you want to display.

To disable the display of subtitles, click *View > Subtitles > None*.

By default, GNOME Videos chooses the same language for the subtitles that you use on your computer.

GNOME Videos automatically loads and displays subtitles if the file that contains them has the same name as the video file. It supports the following subtitle file extensions: `srt`, `asc`, `txt`, `sub`, `smi`, or `ssa`.

19.2   Modifying GNOME Videos Preferences

To modify GNOME Videos preferences, click *Videos > Preferences*.

19.2.1 General Preferences

The General Preferences let you select a network connection speed, specify if media files should be played from the last used position, and change the font and encoding used to display subtitles.

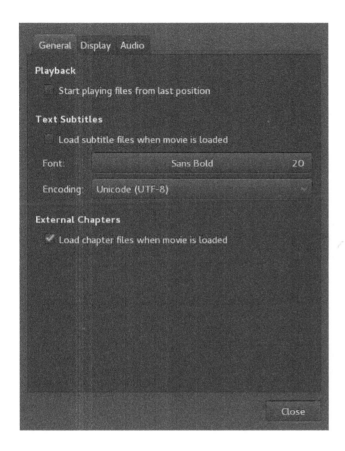

FIGURE 19.2: GNOME VIDEOS GENERAL PREFERENCES

General Preferences include the following:

Playback

Lets you specify whether to start playing the movie from the last position.

Networking

Select network connection speed from the Connection speed drop-down box.

Text Subtitles

Lets you specify whether to load the subtitles automatically, and change the font and encoding used to display the subtitles.

19.2.2 Display Preferences

The Display Preferences let you choose to automatically resize the window when a new video is loaded, change the color balance, and configure visual effects when an audio file is played.

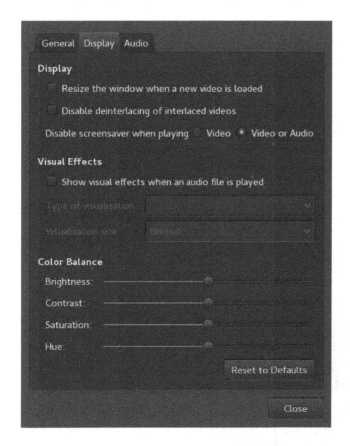

FIGURE 19.3: GNOME VIDEOS DISPLAY PREFERENCES

Display Preferences include the following:

Automatically resize the window when a new video is loaded

Select this option if you want GNOME Videos to automatically resize the window when a new video is loaded.

Disable the screen saver when playing video or audio

Select this option if you want GNOME Videos to automatically disable the desktop screen saver while an audio file is playing.

Visual Effects

You can choose to show visual effects when an audio file is playing, select the type of visualization you want to show, and the visualization size.

Color Balance

Specify the level of color brightness, contrast, saturation, and hue.

19.2.3 Audio Preferences

The Audio Preferences dialog lets you select the audio output type.

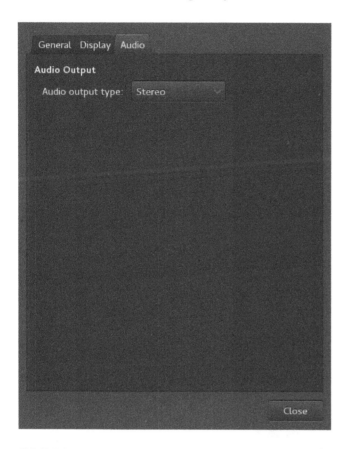

FIGURE 19.4: GNOME VIDEOS AUDIO PREFERENCES

20 Brasero: Burning CDs and DVDs

Brasero is a GNOME program for writing data and audio CDs and DVDs. Start the program from the main menu by clicking *Applications > Sound & Video > Brasero*.

The following sections are a quick introduction on how to create an own CD or DVD.

20.1 Creating a Data CD or DVD

After starting Brasero for the first time, the main window appears as shown in *Figure 20.1*.

FIGURE 20.1: MAIN VIEW OF BRASERO

To create a data CD or DVD, proceed as follows:

1. Click *Data project* or select *Project > New Project > New Data Project*. The project view appears.

2. Drag and drop the desired directories or individual files either from your file manager or by clicking the plus icon. To show your directory structure directly in Brasero, select *View > Show Side Panel* or press F7.

3. Optionally, save the project under a name of your choice with *Project > Save As*.

4. Name your medium. The original label is *Data disc (date)*.

5. Choose the output medium from the pull down menu next to the *Burn* button (CD/DVD or in an ISO image file).

6. Click *Burn*. A new dialog appears, depending on what medium you have selected in the previous step:

   - **CD/DVD.** You can define some parameters, like the burning speed or where to store temporary files. Under *Options* you can also choose whether to burn the image directly, close the session, verify the written data, and others.

   - **ISO Image.** Specify a file name for your ISO image file.

7. Start the process with *Burn*.

20.2 Creating an Audio CD

There are no significant differences between creating an audio CD and creating a data CD. Proceed as follows:

1. Select *Project > New Project > New Audio Project*.

2. Drag and drop the individual audio tracks to the project directory. The audio data must be in WAV or Ogg Vorbis format. Determine the sequence of the tracks by moving them up or down in the project directory.

3. Click *Burn*. A dialog opens.

4. Specify a drive to write to.

5. Click *Properties* to adjust burning speed and other preferences. When burning audio CDs, choose a lower burning speed to reduce the risk of burn errors.

6. Click *Burn*.

20.3 Copying a CD or DVD

To copy a CD or DVD, proceed as follows:

1. Click *Disc Copy* or go to *Project* › *New Project* › *Copy Disc*. The *Copy CD/DVD* dialog opens.

2. Specify the source drive you want to copy.

3. Specify a drive or image file to write to.

4. If necessary, change the burning speed, the temporary directory and other options in *Properties*.

5. Click *Copy*.

20.4 Writing ISO Images

If you already have an ISO image, click *Burn image* or go to *Project* › *New Project* › *Burn Image*. Choose the medium and writer and, if necessary, change parameters by clicking *Properties*. Choose the location of the image file with the pop-up menu labeled *Path*. Start the burning process and click *Burn*.

20.5 Creating a Multisession CD or DVD

Multisession discs can be used to write data in more than one burning session. This is useful, for example, for writing backups that are smaller than the media. In each session, you can add another backup file. One note of interest is that you are not only limited to data CDs or DVDs. You can also add audio sessions in a multisession disc.

To start a new multisession disc, do the following:

1. Start with a data disc first as described in *Section 20.1, "Creating a Data CD or DVD"*. You cannot start with an audio CD session. Make sure that you do not fill up the entire disc, because otherwise you cannot append a new session.

2. Click *Burn*. The window *Disc Burning Setup* opens.

3. Select *Leave the disc open to add other files later* to make the disc multisession capable. Configure other options if needed.

4. Start the burning session with *Burn*.

20.6 For More Information

You can find more information about Brasero at http://www.gnome.org/projects/brasero/.

A Help and Documentation

SUSE® Linux Enterprise Desktop comes with various sources of information and documentation, many of which are already integrated in your installed system:

Desktop Help Center

The help center of the GNOME desktop (Help) provides central access to the most important documentation resources on your system, in searchable form. These resources include online help for installed applications, man pages, info pages, and the SUSE manuals delivered with your product. Learn more in *Section A.1, "Using GNOME Help"*.

Separate Help Packages for Some Applications

When installing new software with YaST, the software documentation is installed automatically in most cases, and usually appears in the help center of your desktop. However, some applications, such as GIMP, may have different online help packages that can be installed separately with YaST and do not integrate into the help centers.

Documentation in `/usr/share/doc`

This traditional help directory holds various documentation files and the release notes for your system. Find more detailed information in *Book "Administration Guide", Chapter 29 "Help and Documentation", Section 29.1 "Documentation Directory"*.

Man Pages and Info Pages for Shell Commands

When working with the shell, you do not need to know the options of the commands by heart. Traditionally, the shell provides integrated help by means of man pages and info pages. Read more in *Book "Administration Guide", Chapter 29 "Help and Documentation", Section 29.2 "Man Pages"* and *Book "Administration Guide", Chapter 29 "Help and Documentation", Section 29.3 "Info Pages"*.

A.1 Using GNOME Help

On the GNOME desktop, to start Help directly from an application, either click the *Help* button or press F1. Both options take you directly to the application's documentation in the help center. However, you can also start Help by clicking *Applications > Utilities > Help*.

FIGURE A.1: MAIN WINDOW OF HELP

To see an overview of available application manuals, click *Go* › *All Documents*.

The menu and the toolbar provide options for navigating and customizing the help center, for searching and for printing contents from Help. The help topics are grouped into categories presented as links. Click one of the links to open a list of topics for that category. To search for an item, enter the search string into the search field at the top of the window.

A.2   Additional Help Resources

In addition to the online versions of the SUSE manuals installed under `/usr/share/doc`, you can also access the product-specific manuals and documentation on the Web. For an overview of all documentation available for SUSE Linux Enterprise Desktop check out your product-specific documentation Web page at http://www.suse.com/documentation/.

If you are searching for additional product-related information, you can also refer to the following Web sites:

- SUSE Knowledgebase [http://www.suse.com/support/kb/]

- SUSE Forums [http://forums.suse.com/]

- SUSE Conversations [http://www.suse.com/communities/conversations/]

- GNOME Documentation Web Site [http://www.gnome.org/]

You can also try general-purpose search engines. For example, use the search terms `Linux CD-RW help` or `LibreOffice file conversion problem` if you were having trouble with the CD burning or with LibreOffice file conversion.

A.3 For More Information

Apart from the product-specific help resources, there is a broad range of information available for Linux topics.

A.3.1 The Linux Documentation Project

The Linux Documentation Project (TLDP) is run by a team of volunteers who write Linux-related documentation (see http://www.tldp.org). The set of documents contains tutorials for beginners, but is mainly focused on experienced users and professional system administrators. TLDP publishes HOWTOs, FAQs, and guides (handbooks) under a free license. Parts of the documentation from TLDP is also available on SUSE Linux Enterprise Desktop.

A.3.1.1 HOWTOs

HOWTOs are usually a short, informal, step-by-step guides to accomplishing specific tasks. HOWTOs can also be found in the package `howto` and are installed under `/usr/share/doc/howto`.

A.3.1.2 Frequently Asked Questions

FAQs (frequently asked questions) are a series of questions and answers. They originate from Usenet newsgroups where the purpose was to reduce continuous reposting of the same basic questions.

A.3.1.3 Guides

Manuals and guides for various topics or programs can be found at http://www.tldp.org/
guides.html. They range from *Bash Guide for Beginners* to *Linux File System Hierarchy* to *Linux
Administrator's Security Guide* . Generally, guides are more detailed and exhaustive than HOW-
TOs or FAQs. They are usually written by experts for experts.

A.3.2 Wikipedia: The Free Online Encyclopedia

Wikipedia is "a multilingual encyclopedia designed to be read and edited by anyone" (see http://
en.wikipedia.org). The content of Wikipedia is created by its users and is published under a
dual free license (GFDL and CC-BY-SA). However, as Wikipedia can be edited by any visitor, it
should be used only as a starting point or general guide. There is much incorrect or incomplete
information in it.

A.3.3 Standards and Specifications

There are various sources that provide information about standards or specifications.

http://www.linux-foundation.org/en/LSB

> The Linux Foundation is an independent nonprofit organization that promotes the distri-
> bution of free and open source software. The organization endeavors to achieve this by
> defining distribution-independent standards. The maintenance of several standards, such
> as the important LSB (Linux Standard Base), is supervised by this organization.

http://www.w3.org

> The World Wide Web Consortium (W3C) is one of the best-known standards organizations.
> It was founded in October 1994 by Tim Berners-Lee and concentrates on standardizing
> Web technologies. W3C promotes the dissemination of open, license-free, and manufac-
> turer-independent specifications, such as HTML, XHTML, and XML. These Web standards
> are developed in a four-stage process in *working groups* and are presented to the public as
> *W3C recommendations* (REC).

http://www.oasis-open.org

> OASIS (Organization for the Advancement of Structured Information Standards) is an in-
> ternational consortium specializing in the development of standards for Web security, e-
> business, business transactions, logistics, and interoperability between various markets.

The Internet Engineering Task Force (IETF) is an internationally active cooperative of researchers, network designers, suppliers, and users. It concentrates on the development of Internet architecture and the smooth operation of the Internet by means of protocols. Every IETF standard is published as an RFC (Request for Comments) and is available free-of-charge. There are six types of RFC: proposed standards, draft standards, Internet standards, experimental protocols, information documents, and historic standards. Only the first three (proposed, draft, and full) are IETF standards in the narrower sense (see http://www.ietf.org/rfc/rfc1796.txt).

The Institute of Electrical and Electronics Engineers (IEEE) is an organization that draws up standards in the areas of information technology, telecommunication, medicine and health care, transport, and others. IEEE standards are subject to a fee.

The ISO Committee (International Organization for Standards) is the world's largest developer of standards and maintains a network of national standardization institutes in over 140 countries. ISO standards are subject to a fee.

The Deutsches Institut für Normung (DIN) is a registered technical and scientific association. It was founded in 1917. According to DIN, the organization is "the institution responsible for standards in Germany and represents German interests in worldwide and European standards organizations."

The association brings together manufacturers, consumers, trade professionals, service companies, scientists and others who have an interest in the establishment of standards. The standards are subject to a fee and can be ordered using the DIN home page.

B Documentation Updates

This chapter lists content changes for this document.

This manual was updated on the following dates:

- Section B.1, "December 2015 (Initial Release of SUSE Linux Enterprise Desktop 12 SP1)"

- Section B.2, "October 2014 (Initial Release of SUSE Linux Enterprise Desktop 12)"

B.1 December 2015 (Initial Release of SUSE Linux Enterprise Desktop 12 SP1)

General

- *Book "Subscription Management Tool for SLES 12 SP1"* is now part of the documentation for SUSE Linux Enterprise Desktop.

- Add-ons provided by SUSE have been renamed to modules and extensions. The manuals have been updated to reflect this change.

- Numerous small fixes and additions to the documentation, based on technical feedback.

- The registration service has been changed from Novell Customer Center to SUSE Customer Center.

- In YaST, you will now reach *Network Settings* via the *System* group. *Network Devices* is gone (https://bugzilla.suse.com/show_bug.cgi?id=867809).

- Updated Evolution documentation to cover Exchange Web Services support (*Chapter 12, Evolution: E-Mailing and Calendaring*).

- Updated Firefox documentation to cover Firefox ESR 38 (*Chapter 16, Firefox: Browsing the Web*).

- Updated GIMP documentation (*Chapter 18, GIMP: Manipulating Graphics*).

Bugfixes

- Fixed inconsistent terminology referring to the Dash of GNOME Shell (from Doc Comments).

B.2 October 2014 (Initial Release of SUSE Linux Enterprise Desktop 12)

General

- Removed all KDE documentation and references because KDE is no longer shipped.

- Removed all references to SuSEconfig, which is no longer supported (Fate #100011).

- Move from System V init to systemd (Fate #310421). Updated affected parts of the documentation.

- YaST Runlevel Editor has changed to Services Manager (Fate #312568). Updated affected parts of the documentation.

- Removed all references to ISDN support, as ISDN support has been removed (Fate #314594).

- Removed all references to the YaST DSL module as it is no longer shipped (Fate #316264).

- Removed all references to the YaST Modem module as it is no longer shipped (Fate #316264).

- Btrfs has become the default file system for the root partition (Fate #315901). Updated affected parts of the documentation.

- The **dmesg** now provides human-readable time stamps in `ctime()`-like format (Fate #316056). Updated affected parts of the documentation.

- syslog and syslog-ng have been replaced by rsyslog (Fate #316175). Updated affected parts of the documentation.

- MariaDB is now shipped as the relational database instead of MySQL (Fate #313595). Updated affected parts of the documentation.

- SUSE-related products are no longer available from http://download.novell.com but from http://download.suse.com. Adjusted links accordingly.

- Novell Customer Center has been replaced with SUSE Customer Center. Updated affected parts of the documentation.

- `/var/run` is mounted as tmpfs (Fate #303793). Updated affected parts of the documentation.

- The following architectures are no longer supported: Itanium and x86. Updated affected parts of the documentation.

- The traditional method for setting up the network with `ifconfig` has been replaced by `wicked`. Updated affected parts of the documentation.

- A lot of networking commands are deprecated and have been replaced by newer commands (usually **ip**). Updated affected parts of the documentation.

  `arp`: `ip neighbor`
  `ifconfig`: `ip addr`, `ip link`
  `iptunnel`: `ip tunnel`
  `iwconfig`: `iw`
  `nameif`: `ip link`, `ifrename`
  `netstat`: `ss`, `ip route`, `ip -s link`, `ip maddr`
  `route`: `ip route`

- Numerous small fixes and additions to the documentation, based on technical feedback.

Changes for This Guide

- Merged the *Application Guide* into this guide.

- Merged the *LibreOffice Quick Start* into this guide.

- Documentation updated from GNOME 2 to GNOME 3. Major user interface changes.

C GNU Licenses

This appendix contains the GNU Free Documentation License version 1.2.

GNU Free Documentation License

Copyright (C) 2000, 2001, 2002 Free Software Foundation, Inc. 51 Franklin St, Fifth Floor, Boston, MA 02110-1301 USA. Everyone is permitted to copy and distribute verbatim copies of this license document, but changing it is not allowed.

0. PREAMBLE

The purpose of this License is to make a manual, textbook, or other functional and useful document "free" in the sense of freedom: to assure everyone the effective freedom to copy and redistribute it, with or without modifying it, either commercially or non-commercially. Secondarily, this License preserves for the author and publisher a way to get credit for their work, while not being considered responsible for modifications made by others.

This License is a kind of "copyleft", which means that derivative works of the document must themselves be free in the same sense. It complements the GNU General Public License, which is a copyleft license designed for free software.

We have designed this License to use it for manuals for free software, because free software needs free documentation: a free program should come with manuals providing the same freedoms that the software does. But this License is not limited to software manuals; it can be used for any textual work, regardless of subject matter or whether it is published as a printed book. We recommend this License principally for works whose purpose is instruction or reference.

1. APPLICABILITY AND DEFINITIONS

This License applies to any manual or other work, in any medium, that contains a notice placed by the copyright holder saying it can be distributed under the terms of this License. Such a notice grants a world-wide, royalty-free license, unlimited in duration, to use that work under the conditions stated herein. The "Document", below, refers to any such manual or work. Any member of the public is a licensee, and is addressed as "you". You accept the license if you copy, modify or distribute the work in a way requiring permission under copyright law.

A "Modified Version" of the Document means any work containing the Document or a portion of it, either copied verbatim, or with modifications and/or translated into another language.

A "Secondary Section" is a named appendix or a front-matter section of the Document that deals exclusively with the relationship of the publishers or authors of the Document to the Document's overall subject (or to related matters) and contains nothing that could fall directly within that overall subject. (Thus, if the Document is in part a textbook of mathematics, a Secondary Section may not explain any mathematics.) The relationship could be a matter of historical connection with the subject or with related matters, or of legal, commercial, philosophical, ethical or political position regarding them.

The "Invariant Sections" are certain Secondary Sections whose titles are designated, as being those of Invariant Sections, in the notice that says that the Document is released under this License. If a section does not fit the above definition of Secondary then it is not allowed to be designated as Invariant. The Document may contain zero Invariant Sections. If the Document does not identify any Invariant Sections then there are none.

The "Cover Texts" are certain short passages of text that are listed, as Front-Cover Texts or Back-Cover Texts, in the notice that says that the Document is released under this License. A Front-Cover Text may be at most 5 words, and a Back-Cover Text may be at most 25 words.

A "Transparent" copy of the Document means a machine-readable copy, represented in a format whose specification is available to the general public, that is suitable for revising the document straightforwardly with generic text editors or (for images composed of pixels) generic paint programs or (for drawings) some widely available drawing editor, and that is suitable for input to text formatters or for automatic translation to a variety of formats suitable for input to text formatters. A copy made in an otherwise Transparent file format whose markup, or absence of markup, has been arranged to thwart or discourage subsequent modification by readers is not Transparent. An image format is not Transparent if used for any substantial amount of text. A copy that is not "Transparent" is called "Opaque".

Examples of suitable formats for Transparent copies include plain ASCII without markup, Texinfo input format, LaTeX input format, SGML or XML using a publicly available DTD, and standard-conforming simple HTML, PostScript or PDF designed for human modification. Examples of transparent image formats include PNG, XCF and JPG. Opaque formats include proprietary formats that can be read and edited only by proprietary word processors, SGML or XML for which the DTD and/or processing tools are not generally available, and the machine-generated HTML, PostScript or PDF produced by some word processors for output purposes only.

The "Title Page" means, for a printed book, the title page itself, plus such following pages as are needed to hold, legibly, the material this License requires to appear in the title page. For works in formats which do not have any title page as such, "Title Page" means the text near the most prominent appearance of the work's title, preceding the beginning of the body of the text.

A section "Entitled XYZ" means a named subunit of the Document whose title either is precisely XYZ or contains XYZ in parentheses following text that translates XYZ in another language. (Here XYZ stands for a specific section name mentioned below, such as "Acknowledgements", "Dedications", "Endorsements", or "History".) To "Preserve the Title" of such a section when you modify the Document means that it remains a section "Entitled XYZ" according to this definition.

The Document may include Warranty Disclaimers next to the notice which states that this License applies to the Document. These Warranty Disclaimers are considered to be included by reference in this License, but only as regards disclaiming warranties: any other implication that these Warranty Disclaimers may have is void and has no effect on the meaning of this License.

2. VERBATIM COPYING

You may copy and distribute the Document in any medium, either commercially or noncommercially, provided that this License, the copyright notices, and the license notice saying this License applies to the Document are reproduced in all copies, and that you add no other conditions whatsoever to those of this License. You may not use technical measures to obstruct or control the reading or further copying of the copies you make or distribute. However, you may accept compensation in exchange for copies. If you distribute a large enough number of copies you must also follow the conditions in section 3.

You may also lend copies, under the same conditions stated above, and you may publicly display copies.

3. COPYING IN QUANTITY

If you publish printed copies (or copies in media that commonly have printed covers) of the Document, numbering more than 100, and the Document's license notice requires Cover Texts, you must enclose the copies in covers that carry, clearly and legibly, all these Cover Texts: Front-Cover Texts on the front cover, and Back-Cover Texts on the back cover. Both covers must also clearly and legibly identify you as the publisher of these copies. The front cover must present the full title with all words of the title equally prominent and visible. You may add other material on the covers in addition. Copying with changes limited to the covers, as long as they preserve the title of the Document and satisfy these conditions, can be treated as verbatim copying in other respects.

If the required texts for either cover are too voluminous to fit legibly, you should put the first ones listed (as many as fit reasonably) on the actual cover, and continue the rest onto adjacent pages.

If you publish or distribute Opaque copies of the Document numbering more than 100, you must either include a machine-readable Transparent copy along with each Opaque copy, or state in or with each Opaque copy a computer-network location from which the general network-using public has access to download using public-standard network protocols a complete Transparent copy of the Document, free of added material. If you use the latter option, you must take reasonably prudent steps, when you begin distribution of Opaque copies in quantity, to ensure that this Transparent copy will remain thus accessible at the stated location until at least one year after the last time you distribute an Opaque copy (directly or through your agents or retailers) of that edition to the public.

It is requested, but not required, that you contact the authors of the Document well before redistributing any large number of copies, to give them a chance to provide you with an updated version of the Document.

4. MODIFICATIONS

You may copy and distribute a Modified Version of the Document under the conditions of sections 2 and 3 above, provided that you release the Modified Version under precisely this License, with the Modified Version filling the role of the Document, thus licensing distribution and modification of the Modified Version to whoever possesses a copy of it. In addition, you must do these things in the Modified Version:

A. Use in the Title Page (and on the covers, if any) a title distinct from that of the Document, and from those of previous versions (which should, if there were any, be listed in the History section of the Document). You may use the same title as a previous version if the original publisher of that version gives permission.

B. List on the Title Page, as authors, one or more persons or entities responsible for authorship of the modifications in the Modified Version, together with at least five of the principal authors of the Document (all of its principal authors, if it has fewer than five), unless they release you from this requirement.

C. State on the Title page the name of the publisher of the Modified Version, as the publisher.

D. Preserve all the copyright notices of the Document.

E. Add an appropriate copyright notice for your modifications adjacent to the other copyright notices.

F. Include, immediately after the copyright notices, a license notice giving the public permission to use the Modified Version under the terms of this License, in the form shown in the Addendum below.

G. Preserve in that license notice the full lists of Invariant Sections and required Cover Texts given in the Document's license notice.

H. Include an unaltered copy of this License.

I. Preserve the section Entitled "History", Preserve its Title, and add to it an item stating at least the title, year, new authors, and publisher of the Modified Version as given on the Title Page. If there is no section Entitled "History" in the Document, create one stating the title, year, authors, and publisher of the Document as given on its Title Page, then add an item describing the Modified Version as stated in the previous sentence.

J. Preserve the network location, if any, given in the Document for public access to a Transparent copy of the Document, and likewise the network locations given in the Document for previous versions it was based on. These may be placed in the "History" section. You may omit a network location for a work that was published at least four years before the Document itself, or if the original publisher of the version it refers to gives permission.

K. For any section Entitled "Acknowledgements" or "Dedications", Preserve the Title of the section, and preserve in the section all the substance and tone of each of the contributor acknowledgements and/or dedications given therein.

L. Preserve all the Invariant Sections of the Document, unaltered in their text and in their titles. Section numbers or the equivalent are not considered part of the section titles.

M. Delete any section Entitled "Endorsements". Such a section may not be included in the Modified Version.

N. Do not retitle any existing section to be Entitled "Endorsements" or to conflict in title with any Invariant Section.

O. Preserve any Warranty Disclaimers.

If the Modified Version includes new front-matter sections or appendices that qualify as Secondary Sections and contain no material copied from the Document, you may at your option designate some or all of these sections as invariant. To do this, add their titles to the list of Invariant Sections in the Modified Version's license notice. These titles must be distinct from any other section titles.

You may add a section Entitled "Endorsements", provided it contains nothing but endorsements of your Modified Version by various parties--for example, statements of peer review or that the text has been approved by an organization as the authoritative definition of a standard.

You may add a passage of up to five words as a Front-Cover Text, and a passage of up to 25 words as a Back-Cover Text, to the end of the list of Cover Texts in the Modified Version. Only one passage of Front-Cover Text and one of Back-Cover Text may be added by (or through arrangements made by) any one entity. If the Document already includes a cover text for the same cover, previously added by you or by arrangement made by the same entity you are acting on behalf of, you may not add another; but you may replace the old one, on explicit permission from the previous publisher that added the old one.

The author(s) and publisher(s) of the Document do not by this License give permission to use their names for publicity for or to assert or imply endorsement of any Modified Version.

5. COMBINING DOCUMENTS

You may combine the Document with other documents released under this License, under the terms defined in section 4 above for modified versions, provided that you include in the combination all of the Invariant Sections of all of the original documents, unmodified, and list them all as Invariant Sections of your combined work in its license notice, and that you preserve all their Warranty Disclaimers.

The combined work need only contain one copy of this License, and multiple identical Invariant Sections may be replaced with a single copy. If there are multiple Invariant Sections with the same name but different contents, make the title of each such section unique by adding at the end of it, in parentheses, the name of the original author or publisher of that section if known, or else a unique number. Make the same adjustment to the section titles in the list of Invariant Sections in the license notice of the combined work.

In the combination, you must combine any sections Entitled "History" in the various original documents, forming one section Entitled "History"; likewise combine any sections Entitled "Acknowledgements", and any sections Entitled "Dedications". You must delete all sections Entitled "Endorsements".

6. COLLECTIONS OF DOCUMENTS

You may make a collection consisting of the Document and other documents released under this License, and replace the individual copies of this License in the various documents with a single copy that is included in the collection, provided that you follow the rules of this License for verbatim copying of each of the documents in all other respects.

You may extract a single document from such a collection, and distribute it individually under this License, provided you insert a copy of this License into the extracted document, and follow this License in all other respects regarding verbatim copying of that document.

7. AGGREGATION WITH INDEPENDENT WORKS

A compilation of the Document or its derivatives with other separate and independent documents or works, in or on a volume of a storage or distribution medium, is called an "aggregate" if the copyright resulting from the compilation is not used to limit the legal rights of the compilation's users beyond what the individual works permit. When the Document is included in an aggregate, this License does not apply to the other works in the aggregate which are not themselves derivative works of the Document.

If the Cover Text requirement of section 3 is applicable to these copies of the Document, then if the Document is less than one half of the entire aggregate, the Document's Cover Texts may be placed on covers that bracket the Document within the aggregate, or the electronic equivalent of covers if the Document is in electronic form. Otherwise they must appear on printed covers that bracket the whole aggregate.

8. TRANSLATION

Translation is considered a kind of modification, so you may distribute translations of the Document under the terms of section 4. Replacing Invariant Sections with translations requires special permission from their copyright holders, but you may include translations of some or all Invariant Sections in addition to the original versions of these Invariant Sections. You may include a translation of this License, and all the license notices in the Document, and any Warranty Disclaimers, provided that you also include the original English version of this License and the original versions of those notices and disclaimers. In case of a disagreement between the translation and the original version of this License or a notice or disclaimer, the original version will prevail.

If a section in the Document is Entitled "Acknowledgements", "Dedications", or "History", the requirement (section 4) to Preserve its Title (section 1) will typically require changing the actual title.

9. TERMINATION

You may not copy, modify, sublicense, or distribute the Document except as expressly provided for under this License. Any other attempt to copy, modify, sublicense or distribute the Document is void, and will automatically terminate your rights under this License. However, parties who have received copies, or rights, from you under this License will not have their licenses terminated so long as such parties remain in full compliance.

10. FUTURE REVISIONS OF THIS LICENSE

The Free Software Foundation may publish new, revised versions of the GNU Free Documentation License from time to time. Such new versions will be similar in spirit to the present version, but may differ in detail to address new problems or concerns. See http://www.gnu.org/copyleft/.

Each version of the License is given a distinguishing version number. If the Document specifies that a particular numbered version of this License "or any later version" applies to it, you have the option of following the terms and conditions either of that specified version or of any later version that has been published (not as a draft) by the Free Software Foundation. If the Document does not specify a version number of this License, you may choose any version ever published (not as a draft) by the Free Software Foundation.

ADDENDUM: How to use this License for your documents

```
Copyright (c) YEAR YOUR NAME.

Permission is granted to copy, distribute and/or modify this document

under the terms of the GNU Free Documentation License, Version 1.2

or any later version published by the Free Software Foundation;

with no Invariant Sections, no Front-Cover Texts, and no Back-Cover

 Texts.

A copy of the license is included in the section entitled "GNU

Free Documentation License".
```

If you have Invariant Sections, Front-Cover Texts and Back-Cover Texts, replace the "with...Texts." line with this:

```
with the Invariant Sections being LIST THEIR TITLES, with the

Front-Cover Texts being LIST, and with the Back-Cover Texts being LIST.
```

If you have Invariant Sections without Cover Texts, or some other combination of the three, merge those two alternatives to suit the situation.

If your document contains nontrivial examples of program code, we recommend releasing these examples in parallel under your choice of free software license, such as the GNU General Public License, to permit their use in free software.

www.ingramcontent.com/pod-product-compliance
Lightning Source LLC
Chambersburg PA
CBHW080410060326

40689CB00019B/4190